MOMENTS OF GRACE

DAILY INSPIRATION FROM ISAIAH TO REVELATION

GERALD O'COLLINS

kevin
mayhew

kevin
mayhew

First published in Great Britain in 2018 by Kevin Mayhew Ltd
Buxhall, Stowmarket, Suffolk IP14 3BW
Tel: +44 (0) 1449 737978 Fax: +44 (0) 1449 737834
E-mail: info@kevinmayhew.com

www.kevinmayhew.com

9 8 7 6 5 4 3 2 1 0

ISBN 978 1 84867 940 5
Catalogue No. 1501575

Cover design by Rob Mortonson
© Images used under licence from Shutterstock Inc.
Typeset by Angela Selfe

Printed and bound in Great Britain

Woodland
CARBON
www.woodlandcarbon.co.uk
KEVIN MAYHEW
Printed on Carbon Captured paper

Contents

Acts of the Apostles

Paul's Letters

First Letter of Peter

Book of Revelation

About the author

Melbourne-born, Gerald O'Collins, SJ, AC, took his PhD at the University of Cambridge before teaching theology at the Pontifical Gregorian University (Rome) from 1973 to 2006. He is now an adjunct professor of Australian Catholic University and research fellow of the University of Divinity (Melbourne). Well known around the world as a visiting lecturer and professor, he has published hundreds of articles in popular and professional journals. He has authored or co-authored 72 books, including most recently, *Saint Augustine on the Resurrection of Christ* (Oxford University Press), *Revelation* (OUP), *Letters to Nevie* (St Paul's Publishing), and *Catholicism: A Very Short Introduction* (new ed., OUP). In 2006 he was created a Companion of the General Division of the Order of Australia (AC), the highest civil honour granted through the Australian government.

Preface

Recently I was chatting about the Holy Trinity with a young priest who had done a doctorate in astrophysics with a Nobel laureate before entering the seminary. 'We live in a space-time world that reflects the Trinity,' he remarked. 'Space, with its three dimensions, diversifies our world, while the one matrix of time unifies our world.' Three persons 'diversify' God, while the 'matrix' of the one divine nature 'unifies' God.

There is obviously a useful analogy to be drawn between (a) space and time, and (b) the three divine persons in one God. I appreciated the force of my friend's insights and comparison. The space-time world forms our total environment in a way that reflects the tripersonal God in whom 'we live and move and have our being' (Acts 17:28).

In presenting God who is one and three, St Patrick (d. around 461 AD) is said to have used the one plant (the Irish shamrock) with trifoliate leaves. A few centuries earlier the North African Tertullian (d. around 220) also introduced material images for the Trinity: for instance, that of a spring, a river, and a canal. One continuous stretch of water is distinguished in a 'tripartite' way, like a flag with three distinct bands of colour, or a triangle containing a circle or surrounded by a circle. These images have obviously been helpful schemes for expressing trinity in unity.

Yet, here as elsewhere, more life-giving force comes by letting the language and images of the Scripture confront us. The word of God continues to be uniquely inspiring and spiritually energising – heart-warming and soul-warming, as another friend of mine puts it.

Take, for instance, the very old blessing that Jewish priests used in the Temple: 'The Lord bless you and keep you; the Lord make his face to shine upon you' (Numbers 6:24, 25). The face of a human being can shine and become radiant. Every now and then we see faces that beam with light and become vividly radiant. That happens also with little children. Their faces light up and shine upon those who hold them in their arms.

That happened long ago in Bethlehem. The face of a tiny child shone upon his parents and those who came to honour him. It was the Lord making his face to shine upon us. The radiant face of the tiny baby in Mary's arms was nothing less than the shining, human face of God.

This book will sample and reflect on biblical passages from Isaiah to the Book of Revelation. Chapters 1-4 will reflect on passages from the Old Testament. Chapters 5-12 take up Matthew's Gospel; chapters 13-17 turn to Mark, chapters 18-23 to Luke, and chapters 24-28 to John. Then chapter 29 ponders passages from the Acts of the Apostles, chapters 31-32 move to St Paul, chapter 33 to 1 Peter, and chapter 34 to Revelation. Some of these reflections will be shorter, some longer. In all cases I hope to bring out for readers the Spirit-filled light and power that the Scriptures embody.

This book is dedicated to three precious people: Chris Mostert, Anne Steinemann and Denis White.

Jesuit Theological College, Parkville, Australia
12 July 2017

OLD TESTAMENT

ONE

Tenderness and Holiness

'Can a woman forget the infant at her breast, or a mother the child of her womb? But should even these forget, I shall never forget you. I have inscribed you on the palms of my hands; your walls are always before my eyes' (Isaiah 49:15, 16 own translation).

Is there any other passage in the entire Bible that uses more tender expressions than these words addressed to the people of Jerusalem? Through the prophet, God adopts one intimate image after another.

God speaks of an infant at a woman's breast, a child in her womb, a name written on the palms of his hands, and a people 'always before my eyes'. It is hard to imagine a gentler, more warm-hearted appeal than this appeal which invokes 'breasts', 'wombs', 'palms of hands', and 'eyes'.

God first puts this passionate cri de coeur negatively. 'Even if a woman were to forget the baby at her breast and fail to cherish the child of her womb, I will never forget you.' Then the protestation of love takes a positive form. 'I have written your name on the palms of my hands. You are always before my eyes.'

Through this tender language, God says to all of us and to each of us: 'You are always intimately present to me.

I cannot take my eyes off you. I cannot stop holding you ever so close – carrying you, loving you, and nourishing you, as a woman does her child.'

In the Book of Leviticus, God appeals to the people, 'be holy, for I am holy' (Leviticus 11:44, 45), an appeal repeated later in the same book (19:2; 20:26) and taken up in the New Testament (1 Peter 1:16).

In recent years (2012-15) many Catholics and other Christians recalled and reflected upon the teaching of the Second Vatican Council, which had taken place 50 years before (1962-5). None of the previous 20 councils of the Church focused attention so resolutely on holiness as an essential characteristic of the Church and all her members.

Of course, a fourth-century council bequeathed to us the creed in which we confess the Church to be 'one, *holy*, catholic, and apostolic'. But the creed did not spell out what it means to be a holy community.

Vatican II, however, had much to say about the holiness of the Church and the vocation of all the baptised to live a life of holiness. Baptism commits every Christian to lead a truly holy existence, set apart for the service of God.

The Christian community is not divided into two classes: a privileged group of chosen souls who enjoy a head start in the matter of holiness, and the rest who muddle along, try to keep the commandments, and avoid sin as much as they can. Christians do not form two classes: an honours class and a pass or fail class.

They are all called to serve God and live genuinely holy lives. They make up together what St Paul calls the temple of the Holy Spirit (1 Corinthians 3:16). Each one of the baptised has received the Holy Spirit, and been blessed and consecrated by the Holy Trinity. Our common call to holiness is rooted and grounded in the life of God, who is Father, Son, and Holy Spirit.

Paul would find it strange to think here of two levels, as if real holiness was reserved to a 'higher' class of Christians, while 'ordinary' goodness was the vocation of 'rank and file' or lower level Christians. To be sure, Paul knew how the followers of Christ have different gifts and different places in society. But he insists that the holy temple of God includes everyone in the community.

Baptism commits all Christians, whatever their position in life, to a genuinely holy existence. Of course, the details of their daily lives remain different, even very different. But it is in and through those different situations that their true holiness or service of God can grow and flourish.

In the Constitution on the Church, the Second Vatican Council described such a life of holiness as building others up with love (*Lumen Gentium*, 39–42). Building others up with love – that can be the most difficult task for those who take to heart the call, 'be holy, for I, the Lord your God, am holy'.

Some years ago, Dan Brown's book, *The Da Vinci Code*, was the talk of the town. That book and the film version gave fresh fame to a medieval building in Southern Scotland, Rosslyn Chapel.

Its chaplain in the late twentieth century had been Fr Roland Walls. After some years Roland left Rosslyn Chapel, went across the road, and founded a religious community. They lived an austere life in a tin shack.

When the project was taking place, Roland and his first companion went off to spend three days in silent prayer 'on retreat'. The director of the retreat asked them to spend the first day reflecting on the fact that 'God loves you'. On the following day their theme was 'you can love God'. For the third day, Roland and his companion were asked to concentrate on the hardest task of all, 'love one another'.

Loving one another is the hardest task of all. It reaches the very heart of our call to holiness.

In a vision of the heavenly throne room, the prophet Isaiah heard seraphs crying out, 'holy, holy, holy is the Lord of hosts; the whole earth is full of his glory' (Isaiah 6:3). The triple 'holy' meant recognising how unique, unimaginable holiness forms a central characteristic of God.

Like Isaiah, we too are invited to acknowledge the wonderful holiness of God. Not only that; we are also called to imitate the divine holiness. That sets the bar very high for the way we should live.

Yet that's what the Old Testament does. It highlights the holiness of God and our vocation to share in that holiness.

So too does the New Testament. The First Letter of Peter simply takes over from Leviticus the divine command: 'You shall be holy, for I am holy'.

Yes, God is supremely holy. And we are all called to let the very holiness of God shape our entire personal existence.

TWO

On Not Delaying and Being Grateful

Among the longest books in the Bible, the Wisdom of Jesus, Son of Sirach (Ben Sira), is filled with wise teaching. Its teaching applies everywhere and to everyone. It provides us with 'a life well lit' – to cite a recent advertisement for lenses.

Ben Sira puts his finger on various basic challenges and recurrent spiritual issues. He begs his reader, for instance: 'Do not delay to turn back to the Lord, and do not postpone it from day to day' (Sirach 5:7).

Sirach knows how prone we human beings are to delay. We are constantly inclined to postpone decisions, especially decisions that are difficult and costly. We can keep putting things off, taking our time, and never really deciding and going into action.

We can so easily procrastinate. That's a very suggestive verb, 'pro-crastinate'. It means indulging the spirit of 'mañana', constantly putting things off until 'cras' or tomorrow arrives, and then putting things off again when tomorrow does arrive.

But with God – not to mention human beings – we cannot afford to delay and put things off day after day.

We cannot afford to miss the moments of grace, those moments when the Lord calls us to stop doing old things and start doing something new.

Some readers will be familiar with three masterpieces featuring the apostle Matthew, painted by Caravaggio and found in a chapel of a church (St Louis of France) in Rome. The first painting depicts Matthew sitting in his tax booth, engaged in the unsavoury work of collecting or extorting taxes. It presents him right at the moment when Christ calls him to leave his disreputable occupation and become a disciple (Matthew 9:9).

There is Matthew sitting at his desk, with light shining on his face. Christ, the Light of the World, is calling him to begin experiencing a 'life well lit' through the lenses of Christ.

It's a moment of glad grace. Matthew cannot afford to delay his decision. He must not postpone matters until tomorrow or the next day. He cannot afford to procrastinate. It is now or never.

I am sure Jesus Ben Sira and Matthew have long ago met in heaven. Perhaps among the things they shared was what Ben Sira wrote more or less two centuries before Matthew came on the human scene. Maybe he congratulated Matthew on not delaying and postponing matters when Jesus stopped to call him.

It was a difficult and costly decision for the tax collector Matthew to make. But he didn't delay. He got up at once, followed Jesus, and never looked back.

What motivation kept Ben Sira going right through his long life? What motivation kept Matthew going as one of the core group of 12 apostles who led the Christian movement as it moved on and out after the first Pentecost? After so many centuries we cannot psychoanalyse at depth Ben Sira and Matthew. But it would be an informed and convincing guess to think that sheer gratitude played a major role in their spiritual mind-set.

Over and over again the Scriptures call for gratitude. In a classical passage found in Deuteronomy (4:32–40), Moses appeals to the people to be grateful to God. There is really so much that they should remember and give thanks for.

God has spoken to them and chosen them as his special people. God has freed them from their slavery in Egypt and is bringing them to the Promised Land. Moses encourages the people to think hard about everything that God has done for them and continues to do for them.

When we think about our lives, yes, there are painful things to remember – mistakes we made and times when others really hurt us. But there is also so much to be grateful for.

Right through life, we have enjoyed the Son of God as our incredible friend and constant companion. Right through life, God has sent us men and women who have proved a blessing to us in great things and small things. They have loved us and set us free to become the people we were called to be.

In the liturgical readings for weekdays in ordinary time, the passage from Deuteronomy 4 has been chosen for the Friday of the eighteenth week in year II. It is followed by a response from Psalm 77 verse 11: 'I will call to mind the deeds of the Lord'.

Yes, let us remember the deeds of the Lord. For the Lord has loved us, guided our lives, and blessed us in so many ways and through so many people.

A proverb that we find in different languages brings to mind one way in which God blesses us. 'God writes straight with crooked lines', or 'God writes straight on crooked lines.'

We human beings provide the crooked lines: the mistakes, the sins, the failures, and the rest. But God can turn these things to good. God consistently makes something of our sinful schemes and human blunders.

A complicated story about Rebekah conspiring to trick old Isaac into giving his special blessing to Jacob and not to his eldest son, Esau, contains some crooked lines (Genesis 26:34–28:9). Jacob joins his mother in writing the crooked lines. But eventually God turns it all to good, and from Jacob is descended Jesus himself.

What we write in creating the story of our lives can go up and down, and we end up with pages of crooked lines. Repeatedly, the Bible shows us people like Rebekah and Jacob doing just that. They do not move straight ahead in their lives but write their crooked lines.

But the Bible also shows our infinitely wise and loving God making something positive and even wonderful out of those mistakes and sins. Our God can and does write straight on our crooked lines.

THREE

Praising and Thanking God

'Then the prophet Miriam, Aaron's sister, took a tambourine in her hand; and all the women went out after her with tambourines and with dancing. And Miriam sang to them: "Sing to the Lord, for he has triumphed gloriously; horse and rider he has thrown into the sea"' (Exodus 15:20, 21).

According to the Old Testament, women typically led victory songs and dancing in celebration of triumphs. When David, for instance, returned from slaying the Philistine warrior, Goliath, 'women came out of all the towns of Israel, singing and dancing, with tambourines, with songs of joy, and with three-stringed instruments' (1 Samuel 18:6).

After the people were delivered from slavery in Egypt, women, led by the prophetess Miriam, honoured with song and dance, not Moses their human leader, but God the warrior king. In what has been recognised as one of the oldest passages in the Bible, Miriam and the other women praised God as their liberator.

The Jewish midwives had been the first to resist the Pharaoh. It was they who saved the life of the infant Moses (Exodus 1:15–2:10). It was fitting that women should have the last word when the liberation from the Egyptians was completed.

The Easter vigil features the song of Miriam and her companions. With something of their joy in our hearts, let us sing the song of praise and thanksgiving.

The psalms repeatedly praise and thank God, who has not only made the universe but also faithfully delivered his people from all kinds of dangers and evils. To drive home the theme of praise and thanksgiving, the Book of the Psalms closes with six psalms that praise God our Creator and Saviour.

Psalm 149 picks up this language and invites all the people of Israel: 'Let them praise his [God's] name with dancing, making melody to him with tambourine and lyre' (Psalm 149:3). This psalm identifies two musical instruments: tambourines and lyres.

The climax of the final six psalms, Psalm 150 runs through more instruments of ancient orchestras, naming trumpets, lutes, harps, tambourines, 'strings and pipe', and 'loud clashing cymbals'. It invites everyone to 'dance' and 'praise the Lord' – for the 'mighty firmament' he has created and for 'his mighty deeds', above all the deliverance from Egypt that the Israelites remembered and celebrated.

In a crescendo of applause and admiration, the powerful hymn that is Psalm 150 calls on all living creatures. Let them pay homage to God in a sacred concert that will never end:

Praise the Lord!
Praise God in his sanctuary; praise him in his
mighty firmament!
Praise him for his mighty deeds; praise him
according to his surpassing greatness!
Praise him with trumpet sound; praise him with
lute and harp!
Praise him with tambourine and dance; praise him
with strings and pipe!
Praise him with clanging cymbals; praise him
with loud clashing cymbals!
Let everything that breathes praise the Lord!
Praise the Lord!   *Psalm 150*

Many hymns, ancient and modern, glorify God who is
all-good, all-powerful, all-wise, and, let us not forget, all-
beautiful. Praising God means 'telling out' the greatness
of the Lord.

The hymn of the Blessed Virgin Mary, the 'Magnificat'
(Luke 1:46–55), in the words of Bishop Timothy Dudley-
Smith, set to the music of Walter Greatorex, opens: 'Tell
out, my soul, the greatness of the Lord!' Try singing this
setting of the 'Magnificat' quietly to yourself, and your
heart will be warmed.

Breaking into songs of praise expresses the truth
of who God is and what God has done for each of us.
Remembering how gloriously wonderful and wonderfully
glorious God is, we can turn to that splendid hymn,
'O God, beyond all praising, we worship you today'.

Another hymn, 'How great thou art', summons us to sing to God who has created the world. Through bleeding and dying on the cross, Jesus has taken away sin and become 'my Saviour God'.

Christian hymn books supply us with the language and the tunes that we can quietly sing to ourselves. Older hymns can serve us well: 'All people that on earth do dwell', 'Holy God, we praise your name', 'Immortal, invisible, God only wise', 'Praise God from whom all blessings flow', and 'Praise, my soul, the King of heaven'.

Newer hymns, like 'All the ends of the earth' and 'Glory and praise to our God', also let us join the psalmists in glorifying and giving thanks to God. Our imagination can take us back many centuries, to Miriam and her companions singing and dancing with joy as they honoured their divine Deliverer.

Constantly praising and thanking God establishes the only truly appropriate lifestyle for believers. In its picturesque way, the Book of Revelation calls on Christians to unite themselves with the marvellous liturgy that will be the life of heaven. They should join their voices to the universal song of praise offered to 'the one who is seated on the throne': 'You are worthy, our Lord and God, to receive glory and honour and power, for you created all things, and by your will they existed and were created'. They should 'sing a new song' to the Lamb of God, whose 'blood . . . ransomed for God saints from every tribe and language and people and nation' (Revelation 4:10; 5:9).

This universal praise given to God and to the Lamb is then drawn together. 'Every creature in heaven and on earth' sings: 'To the one seated on the throne and to the Lamb be blessing and honour and glory and might forever and ever' (Revelation 5:13).

Miriam and her fellow dancers, the psalms, Christian hymns, and the Book of Revelation all leave us with the question: how much do I praise God, day by passing day? Constantly glorifying and giving thanks to our loving Lord will let us grow spiritually and deliver us from a false centring on self. By centring on God through prayers, songs, and lives of praise, we will do what we are created for and find the only happiness that will fill our lives forever.

FOUR

Jesus the New Law

For 2000 years now, the psalms have formed *the* prayer book for Christians. The psalms feature constantly in the celebration of the Eucharist and the other sacraments. Hundreds of thousands of Christians recite or sing the psalms every day in the divine office. The public and private prayer of Christians is unthinkable without the use of the psalms.

In his first volume of *Jesus of Nazareth*, Pope Benedict XVI shared some thoughts about the psalms. He called Psalm 119 (at 176 verses by far the longest of the psalms) an 'outburst of joy and gratitude' for the gift of God's law (p. 266). This great gift gave the Israelites their identity as God's people. The law provided them with knowledge of the divine will and set them on the right path, the path of life. Psalm 119 repeatedly expresses their joy at knowing God's will and their praise to God for the privilege of living in accordance with the divine will. The law that God had given them through Moses proved nothing less than that: the very heart of their faith.

Since it is so long, Psalm 119 introduces various synonyms for the law: 'decrees', 'commandments', 'precepts', 'ordinances', 'statutes', 'instruction', 'word', 'promise', and 'will'. These terms function as elegant variations, as we can see in what the psalmist says in verses 162 to 167:

> I rejoice at your *word* like one who finds great spoil.
> I hate and abhor falsehood, but I love your *law*.
> Seven times a day I praise you for your righteous *ordinances*.
> Great peace have those who love your *law*,
> nothing can make them stumble.
> I hope for your salvation, O Lord, and I fulfil your *commandments*.
> My soul keeps your *decrees*; I love them
> exceedingly (emphasis added).

In his letters, St Paul has much to say about God's gift of the law – not least that Christ is 'the end of the law' (Romans 10:4). Here the apostle means the goal to which the law has been leading and pointing. Jesus takes over from the law. He is the law for Christians. He is the great gift of God to his people.

What Paul writes may allow us to put the name of Jesus into the psalm, and pray accordingly to the Father about Jesus:

> I rejoice at your Jesus like one who finds great spoil.
> I hate and abhor falsehood, but I love your Jesus.
> Seven times a day I praise you for your
> righteous Jesus

Great peace have those who love your Jesus;
nothing can make them stumble.
I hope for your salvation, O Lord, and I fulfil
your Jesus.
My soul keeps your Jesus; I love him exceedingly.

By speaking in this way about Jesus in prayer addressed to God the Father, we are in fact retrieving a life-giving practice from the early period of Christianity. For centuries, ancient Christians constantly understood the psalms in ways that brought Jesus into the picture.

This meant using the psalms as a way of *praying to the Father about Jesus.* This practice worked in a lively way for the longest of all the psalms. We can follow suit with Psalm 119, substituting the name of Jesus for 'the law' and its numerous synonyms.

Let me give another example of how this psalm can enter our prayer by introducing the name of Jesus:

See, I have longed for your Jesus [replacing
'precepts']; in your righteousness give me life.
Let your steadfast love come to me, O Lord,
your salvation according to your Jesus
[replacing 'promise'].
Then I shall have an answer for those who taunt
me, for I trust in your Jesus [replacing 'word'].
I find my delight in your Jesus [replacing
'commandments'], because I love [him].

Psalm 119:40–42, 47

Yes, Psalm 119 was originally an 'outburst of joy and gratitude' for the gift of God's law. But in the prayer of Christians it became an outburst of joy and gratitude for the wonderful gift of Jesus. What might seem at first sight a tediously long psalm can be refreshed and revitalised by using it to speak to the Father in praise of Jesus.

MATTHEW'S GOSPEL

FIVE

Joseph, the Magi and the Shepherds

I first learnt about St Joseph from some nuns and from my father's youngest brother. Followers of St Mary of the Cross (better known as St Mary MacKillop), the Sisters of St Joseph taught me in primary school. They had his statue in their convent and his caring concern for others in their heart.

A medical doctor, Uncle Joe enjoyed a busy medical practice but always found time for me. He taught me how to play golf, lent me his dinner jacket for the ball that crowned the social season at the high school I attended, and cheerfully encouraged whatever projects engaged my attention. His constant kindness led me to think more about the great saint whose name he bore.

We may feel disappointed that we know so little about Joseph. None of the Gospels records anything he said. But we learn from Matthew's Gospel what he did when Jesus was conceived and born. There's an old saying: 'actions speak louder than words'. The actions of Joseph spoke loud and strong; his actions spoke of his goodness and love louder than any words he could have uttered.

We first meet Joseph when facing a most painful situation. He discovered that Mary, his fiancée, was expecting a baby. He did not yet know how she had come to be pregnant. From the point of view of society at that time, she had disgraced her own family, insulted her future husband's family, and committed an offence that could lead her to be stoned to death.

But Joseph was a 'just man', and wanted to do his best in a situation that was nothing short of a nightmare. He planned to save the woman he loved by secretly divorcing her (Matthew 1:18, 19). In Matthew's Gospel, 'just' and 'justice' would prove to be a significant theme – not least in the Sermon on the Mount. There Jesus declared 'blessed' those 'who hunger and thirst after justice' (Matthew 5:6). Joseph had already proved himself a role model for those who want to live a 'just' life.

God blessed Joseph by sending an 'angel of the Lord' to let him know what had happened. It was through the power of the Holy Spirit that Mary had become pregnant. Joseph was to give the name of Jesus to her son, who would do nothing less than 'save his people from their sins' and show himself to be 'Emmanuel' or 'God with us' (Matthew 1:20–23).

After the Christ Child is born and the Magi have paid their homage, the 'angel of the Lord' returns to warn Joseph about the murderous plans of Herod the Great. Joseph reacts at once and under cover of night takes the Infant Jesus and Mary away to safety in Egypt.

When Herod dies, the 'angel of the Lord' again appears to Joseph and tells him to return to the Holy Land. Eventually Joseph follows further instructions from God and heads for Galilee to settle himself, Mary, and Jesus no longer in Bethlehem but in a safer place, Nazareth (Matthew 2:13–15, 19–23).

The First Letter of John sums up love as being not a matter of word or speech but of truth and action (1 John 3:18). That could be a description of Joseph. Right through the two opening chapters of Matthew's Gospel, he never makes a speech. In fact, he does not say even one word. It is in action that he shows his love for the Christ Child and for Mary.

Once we move to later chapters of Matthew's Gospel, Joseph drops almost completely out of sight. After Jesus has started his ministry, the people of his hometown, Nazareth, react to him with disbelief. Jesus has grown up among them, and now they find him preaching and working miracles. Yet as far as they are concerned, he is simply 'the son of the carpenter' (Matthew 13:55).

What Matthew says about the profession of Joseph has inspired scenes that painters like Sir John Millais have made familiar. Jesus works away in a carpentry shop and learns the trade from Joseph. Some scholars have been quick to point out that the Greek word *tektōn*, while often translated as 'carpenter', could easily have carried the meaning of 'builder'. Yet it could be more significant to move beyond words and meanings and ask the wider question: what did Jesus learn from Joseph?

Growing up in a uniquely holy home in Nazareth, Jesus found in Joseph a wonderful role model. Day after day, Joseph showed Jesus what it was to be a real man, a devoted husband, and a loving father.

In his preaching, Jesus was to speak about God as 'Abba', 'Daddy' or 'Father dear'. He would tell one of his greatest stories about the loving father of two sons, the younger one who goes off to waste his money in high living and the other a self-righteous prig who stays at home but remains unhappy with the blessings he receives. To illustrate how God can never take his eyes off any of us and cares for each of us in all our needs, Jesus pointed out that no good father would dream of playing nasty tricks on his children. A round loaf of bread could resemble a stone, and dried fish could look like snakeskin. But what loving father would dream of passing his children a stone when they asked for bread or snakeskin when they asked for fish (Matthew 7:9, 10)?

When Jesus spoke about the way in which good human fathers behave, and preached the love of his heavenly Father, we glimpse here and there what he had experienced over the years in Nazareth. He enjoyed a unique mother in the Blessed Virgin Mary, and he also enjoyed a unique father in that 'just' man, Joseph. It was much more than techniques of carpentry or building that Jesus learned from Joseph. By experiencing day by day the fatherly love of Joseph, he saw a reflection of what his heavenly Father is like. By constantly caring for

Mary and her Child and by working day in and day out to put bread on their table, Joseph showed his intense love for Jesus and Mary. He could not take his eyes off them. Right there at home in Nazareth, he provided Jesus with a human image of the loving, heavenly Father who is our God.

At Christmas time we visit cribs in churches, schools, homes, and other places. The Christ Child and Mary his mother normally seize our attention. But we might also pause to focus for a moment on the figure of Joseph. In the plan of God, the safety of Mary and her Child depended upon Joseph. Without him, Mary would at best have become a permanent outcast in her society. Given the rules of Jewish society in those times, Joseph's acceptance of his mission was breathtaking. He worked with Mary to safeguard and educate the Son of God who came among us as a tiny baby. His courageous and self-forgetting love was nothing less than heroic.

I remain lastingly grateful to the Sisters of St Joseph and my uncle Joe for setting me a long time ago on the road to know and value more and more a remarkable human being. Joseph remained an utterly righteous and faithful husband towards Mary. He was also a simply wonderful father to Jesus. In being all that, Joseph showed Jesus and shows us what God is truly like.

At first glance the Magi in Matthew's nativity story (2:1–12) and the shepherds in Luke's nativity story (2:8–20) hardly pair off together. The shepherds may not be totally destitute, but they belong with the poor who struggle to survive. They sleep rough at night, as they guard their sheep under the stars. Economically they rate nowhere near the Magi, who have the resources to travel from a distant country to Bethlehem and bring expensive gifts for the newborn Christ Child. The shepherds bring no gift to the manger but only themselves.

Moreover, the Magi are Gentiles, and not Jews like the shepherds. Admittedly, their way of life makes it impossible for the shepherds to keep all the regulations of the law that God has given to his people. Religiously the shepherds remain on the fringes of Jewish society. Yet, unlike the Magi, they are insiders, not Gentile outsiders.

If we set our minds to it, further differences emerge. A short walk across the countryside let the shepherds find the Christ Child lying in a manger in Bethlehem. They were already living and working in that region (Luke 2:8). The Magi, however, prompted by a strange star they observed at its rising, travelled for many days or even some months before they reached the goal of their journey, the newborn King of the Jews. Distance and time kept the shepherds and the Magi apart when they moved to keep their rendezvous with the Christ Child.

Yet the Magi and the shepherds stand together, and not least for being disadvantaged and needing help. The Magi live in another country, and do not know the inspired Scriptures. The chief priests and scribes have studied their Scriptures. Through King Herod they can direct their exotic visitors from the East towards Bethlehem. That is where the prophet Micah has placed the birth of the Ruler who will shepherd his people. In their search for the newborn King, the Magi have the benefit only of a strange star that they glimpse at its rising (Matthew 2:2) and then, much later, on the road from Jerusalem to Bethlehem (Matthew 2:9).

The shepherds – unlike Elizabeth, Zechariah, Joseph, Simeon, Anna, and, above all, Mary herself – cannot be called devout and observant Jews. Religiously they are marginal people who must watch, day and night, over their flock. The shepherds need an angel of the Lord, backed up with a multitude of other angels singing the praises of God, to stir them into leaving their sheep and heading for Bethlehem.

What holds the Magi and the shepherds together is the way that, despite their disadvantages, they rise at once to the occasion. They respond immediately to the call and the chance they have been given from heaven: through a star in the case of the Magi and through angelic visitors in the case of the shepherds.

The Magi, in particular, take advantage of the very limited chances they have been given and finally reach the journey's end: to the Child who is the King of the Jews. Before that, when they arrive in Jerusalem, not only King Herod but also the whole city feel alarmed at what the Magi say about their search for this newborn king (Matthew 2:3). Yet, even though the priests, the scribes, and others know the Scriptures, in particular the prophecy of Micah about the location of the Messiah's birth, none of them joins the Magi in going a few miles from Jerusalem to Bethlehem. Those with decisive advantages can fail to make use of their chances.

In the nativity season it is worth looking carefully at the figures of the shepherds and the Magi who surround our Christmas cribs. We might ask ourselves: how did they get here to worship our Lord and Saviour, the newborn Christ Child? If we feel that life's lottery has given us few advantages, we can think of the poor shepherds and the rich Magi. In their different ways, the two groups emerge from the Christmas story as those who made the very best of the limited possibilities they had been given.

Whether we come from a distance (like the Magi) or travel only a few miles (like the shepherds), there is always room for us at the manger. O come let us adore our newborn King and Redeemer! No matter where we start from, what counts is using our chance to kneel before the baby lying in the crib or nestling in the arms of Mary.

Brothers, Beatitudes, Perfection and Forgiveness

Individual words play a crucial part in appreciating what the Gospel writers want to convey to their readers. If we are attuned to this feature of Matthew, we will find a lovely message about becoming brothers (and sisters) in the new family that Jesus creates.

Matthew 4:18–22 (on the right) more or less follows, even word for word, what Mark 1:16–20 (on the left) has already reported about the call of the first disciples:

As Jesus passed along the Sea of Galilee, he saw Simon and his brother Andrew casting a net into the sea – for they were fishermen. And Jesus said to them, 'Follow me and I will make you fish for people.' And immediately they left their nets and followed him. As he went a little farther, he saw James son of Zebedee and his brother John, who were in their boat mending the nets. Immediately he called them; and they left their father Zebedee in the boat with the hired men, and followed him.	As he walked by the Sea of Galilee, he saw *two brothers*, Simon, who is called Peter, and Andrew his brother, casting a net into the sea – for they were fishermen. And he said to them, 'Follow me, and I will make you fish for people.' Immediately they left their nets and followed him. As he went from there, he saw *two other brothers*, James son of Zebedee and his brother John, in the boat with their father Zebedee, mending their nets, and he called them. Immediately they left the boat and their father, and followed him.

I have put in italics a significant addition that Matthew has twice made to the text of Mark. Matthew writes of Jesus seeing 'two brothers' (Peter and Andrew) and then seeing 'two other brothers' (James and John). That is what we read early in Matthew's Gospel about Jesus seeing and calling two sets of brothers.

At the end of his Gospel, Matthew gives a message to Mary Magdalene and her companion: 'Go and tell my brothers to go to Galilee; there they will see me' (Matthew 28:10). In Matthew's Gospel, the story begins with Jesus seeing and recruiting two sets of brothers in Galilee. The story ends with those two sets of brothers, along with their seven other companions, seeing the risen Jesus on a mountain in Galilee and being commissioned by him to bring the good news to the whole world (Matthew 28:16–20).

Simon Peter and Andrew began life as blood brothers in the same home. So too did James and John. Both sets of brothers find their final destiny in the new family of the risen Jesus, along with their other brothers and sisters in God's worldwide community. 'Fishing for people' is now clarified as being commissioned by the risen Lord to preach the good news everywhere. That mission will bring together men and women who will follow Jesus and show brotherly-sisterly love to one another in a fellowship that holds fast to Jesus and the truth he has revealed (Revelation 19:10).

In chapter 33 of this book, we will see how The First Letter of Peter encouraged brotherly-sisterly love in the new family that Jesus had founded. I don't know whether Matthew ever read that letter but, if he did, he would have been very pleased to see how it filled out what he had suggested.

The beatitudes (Matthew 5:1–12) summarise the whole way of life that Jesus proclaimed during the three years or so of his earthly ministry. The beatitudes describe the best way to live – in fact, the only way truly worth following. They hold out to us the greatest good imaginable, the kingdom of God. In a concise form they pull together what Jesus announced about the rule of God that is already engaged with our world and that will bring everything to a glorious conclusion.

In calling us to share in his kingdom, Jesus names as truly blessed eight classes of people: the poor in spirit, those who mourn, the meek, those who hunger and thirst after righteousness, the merciful, the pure of heart, and those who are persecuted because they embrace a truly righteous existence.

There in a nutshell is our way for living and for advancing the kingdom of God. May this programme never go out of fashion or disappear from view! We will be blessed if we take in these words of Jesus and, with infectious enthusiasm, set ourselves to live out what he proposed.

Nowadays, advertising copywriters dress up words brilliantly. They are in the business of selling us all kinds of products, good, bad, and indifferent. Whatever the real value of the products, the advertisements can have a useful impact by making us more sensitive to words and the differences between them.

As we saw in Chapter 1 above, the First Letter of Peter echoes passages where the Lord God speaks in the Book of Leviticus by telling its readers, 'You shall be holy, for I am holy' (1 Peter 1:16). In the Gospel of Matthew, Jesus puts a similar invitation but by saying, 'be perfect, therefore, as your heavenly Father is perfect' (Matthew 5:48).

Is there any difference between aiming to be holy and aiming to be perfect? What word should we prefer: holiness or perfection?

St Teresa of Avila wrote a famous and enduringly valuable book, *The Way of Perfection*. Yet the Apostles' Creed speaks of believing in the Church as being 'the *holy* catholic Church', not in 'the *perfect* catholic Church'. The Nicene Creed professes faith in the 'one, *holy*, catholic, and apostolic Church'.

The Second Vatican Council followed the language of the creeds. In its Constitution on the Church, *Lumen Gentium* ('the light of the nations'), the Council published a now famous chapter about all baptised Christians being called to lives of holiness (nos. 39–42).

The words 'holiness' and 'perfection' both appear in the inspired Scriptures. Both words have been used in the worship and teaching of the Church. They have a rich background and a broad range of meanings.

We may think of our lives as following Christ's way of perfection. Or we may find that the call to holiness brings us closer to the truth of God revealed and reflected in our lives. At the end of the day, the choice of language does not matter very much.

What matters is that we constantly let the grace of Our Lord help us listen to that call to holiness and follow that way of perfection. Christ is the one who directs our response, enlightens our lives, and gives lasting significance to our journey.

We are not yet fully and truly holy or fully and truly perfect. We are only following the way of perfection and listening for the call to holiness. May the good Lord always keep us walking that 'camino' and listening to that call.

Unless we embrace this way of seeing life, the alternative adds up to a bleak and empty existence, evoked by the words of a great poet, Kevin Hart: 'Another day with nothing to say for itself'.

Some years ago, I became hooked on a series of Bible films, directed by an Italian, Luca Bernabei, and shot in Morocco. Several of these films featured outstanding actors and actresses, like Diana Rigg.

The series started with Noah and took you right through to Paul. When Bernabei came to the patriarch Joseph, he filmed with expertise the scene when Joseph forgave his brothers for what they had done to him by selling him into slavery. Taken off to Egypt, Joseph had become very powerful under the Pharaoh.

Joseph's brothers came to Egypt and sat with him around the same table. The camera moved from one trembling face to another. The brothers could not believe what they had just heard. Joseph had forgiven them all (Genesis 45:1–15).

Their father Jacob was very old. The brothers remained terrified that, when their father died, Joseph would finally punish them for that they had done to him. Yes, for the moment he had buried the hatchet. Yet he must have carefully marked the spot. He would dig up the hatchet and take revenge on them. But with tears Joseph assured his brothers that he had truly forgiven them.

The story of Joseph and his brothers, whether we read it in the Bible or see it on the screen, brings out powerfully an important lesson. It is difficult, even extremely difficult, for human beings to forgive one another.

Looking back over our own lives, we can see the faces of people whom we have hurt and harmed. It is hard to imagine that they could forgive us. There could also be people who have hurt and harmed us. It is hard to imagine imitating the patriarch Joseph and our forgiving them truly.

That is why I treasure the story of Joseph and his brothers. Real forgiveness can seem unimaginable. But it does happen. God can make it happen. With the Lord's help, we can bury our hatchets and truly forget where we buried them.

Jesus asked us to pray: 'forgive us our trespasses as we forgive those who trespass against us' (Matthew 6:12 own translation). Jesus never said that it was easy to put forgiveness into practice. But with the grace of God, we can become forgiving people.

SEVEN

Treasure, A Feast and Awesome Holiness

' . . . store up for yourselves treasure in heaven . . . where your treasure is, there your heart will be also' (Matthew 6:20, 21).

You don't need to be an opera fan to know that Italian is a language of warm, human affection. In Italian, one affectionate way of addressing a person whom you love is to call that person 'treasure (*tesoro*)'. To be sure, among English-speakers, I have heard a few of them calling a person of whom they are very fond 'treasure'. But '*tesoro*' summons up even more affection. It exudes deep love.

Jesus speaks of storing up treasure in heaven. That's where our heart should be – in heaven where we store up treasure.

What will make heaven heavenly? It will be Jesus himself. Heaven will be living with Jesus in supreme and lasting happiness. He will be our treasure, our heavenly treasure.

We might pray: 'O Jesus, you are my treasure. O Jesus, you will be my wonderful and everlasting treasure. O Jesus, *tesoro mio*, I love you. My heart is with you.'

In the course of meeting with a centurion who wants his sick servant to be healed, Jesus expresses great admiration for the soldier's faith and interjects a wonderful promise: 'Many will come from east and west and will eat with Abraham and Isaac and Jacob in the kingdom of heaven' (Matthew 8:11).

It's an encouraging promise for all of us who come from east or west (and from north or south) and who hope to share in the final feast of the divine kingdom. But someone utterly central is missing in the picture: namely, Jesus himself. He doesn't speak of 'the many' taking their places 'with me' or 'with the Son of Man' at God's table, only of Abraham, Isaac, and Jacob. But, if there's no Jesus, there will be no kingdom of heaven.

I don't want anyone to be excluded or forgotten. But I do want to share that final feast with Jesus. No Jesus, no feast in the kingdom of God.

Happily, later in Matthew's Gospel we find Jesus promising his own presence in the heavenly feast to come (Matthew 25:1–10; 26:29). So we can pray: 'May your kingdom come; may your heavenly feast come, when we will take our place with you, home with you at last.'

Recently the TV screen showed me an ad for a new brand of car: 'Desire is everything. Luxury is everything. Exhilaration is everything.' The promise Jesus made engages us differently and could prompt us to say, 'The desire for your kingdom is everything. The luxury of being with you is everything. The exhilaration of sharing the final feast with you will be everything.'

Biblical scholars commonly hold that Matthew used Mark's Gospel as one of his main sources. It's always interesting to see what Matthew does with the text that Mark provides.

Sometimes Matthew trims down what Mark has written and gives us a shorter version of some story. That's true when we compare Matthew's story of two men in the land of the Gerasenes possessed by fierce demons (8:28–34) with what we read in Mark 5:1–20.

Mark took 20 verses to tell the story. Matthew uses only seven. By leaving out considerable detail, Matthew shows us what he really wants to highlight.

One feature that comes through loud and clear in Matthew's account of the two possessed men being delivered from their demons is the awesome holiness of Jesus. The demons felt the presence of that awesome holiness. And so too did the people of the district.

The demons drove the two possessed men into the presence of Jesus and began shouting: 'What do you want with us, Son of God? Have you come here to torture us before the time?' Then the demons pleaded with Jesus to banish them from his presence, even if that meant being sent to live in a herd of pigs.

At the end of the story, 'the whole town came out to meet Jesus. When they saw him, they begged him to leave their neighbourhood.' That's an extraordinary reaction to what Jesus has just done in liberating two people possessed by demons. It's not just a few people, but 'the whole town' who come out to meet Jesus. They don't drive him away; they don't attempt to do Jesus any harm. But they beg him to leave town. They are afraid of Jesus; he frightens them; he's too dangerous to have around.

Like the demons, the people of the district found the presence of Jesus unbearable. They too wanted him to depart and leave them alone. What's gone wrong?

Jesus is the holy one of God. He is in person the frightening and fascinating divine mystery. The people of the town know that they are in the presence of the holy mystery of God. The awesome holiness and power of Jesus are too much for them to bear. They feel only the frightening part of that mystery. They don't find Jesus to be fascinating.

They are afraid of Jesus but not fascinated by him. They are only half way there in opening themselves to the holy mystery of God that is Jesus himself.

May we come to feel the complete holy mystery revealed in Jesus! May we find Jesus to be frightening, yes, but also fascinating! The holiness and power of Jesus should frighten us, but we should also find him utterly fascinating. And then we will never ask him to leave our neighbourhood.

The reaction of the Gerasenes proved very different from the way in which the founder of the Jesuit order, St Ignatius Loyola, reacted when he came into the presence of the awesomely holy Jesus. Ignatius decided to serve Jesus for the rest of his life.

Ignatius spoke of exercising a loving reverence or reverential love towards the person of Jesus. He wanted others to join him in praising, *reverencing*, and serving Our Lord.

Ignatius would say to us, 'Don't run away from the presence of the awesomely holy Jesus. Don't ask him to leave you alone. But be very glad to stay in the presence of Jesus, and do so with reverential love or loving reverence'.

In a powerful way, Mark's Gospel tells us what happened when Jesus visited the land of the Gerasenes. But we can be grateful also to Matthew, who centres on the awesomely holy Jesus, the One whom we should follow with loving reverence or reverential love.

EIGHT

Being Called, Patches, Skins and Violence

In the church of St Louis in Rome, you can enjoy the wonderful painting by Caravaggio that pictures the call of the apostle Matthew (Matthew 9:9–13), and which I have already mentioned in Chapter 2. On the right, Jesus stretches out his arm in a way that evokes the Sistine Chapel and Michelangelo's depiction of the creation of Adam. On the left, Matthew sits at his table with light shining on his face. He has recognised and now reflects the divine Light that has come into the world. Behind the extended arm of Christ, there is an open window; its woodwork takes the shape of a cross.

In a brilliant way, Caravaggio associates the creation of the world with the divine Light flooding into human history at the incarnation, and then with the call of Matthew to follow Christ who will die on a cross of wood. Caravaggio succeeds in bringing together the events of creation, incarnation and crucifixion.

Matthew himself was blessed in three marvellous ways. He was created and brought into existence by God. He saw and accepted the divine Light that shone from the face of Christ. He was also called to a mission that would climax with the crucifixion and, later, with his own sharing in the passion of his Master.

Caravaggio's painting of Matthew's call links three basic and enormous blessings that also shape our lives. We have been created and brought into existence. We have seen the glory of God on the face of Christ. We are all called to become missionaries to the world, sharers in a mission that involves the passion of Christ and our own passion.

When I read what the Gospels report from the preaching of Jesus, I keep an eye out for the new images he uses. Sometimes, of course, he uses images that you find in the Old Testament. He is likely to give these traditional images a fresh twist. Take, for example, the image of Israel as the vineyard of God (Isaiah 5:1–7), and see what Jesus does with that image in his parable of the vineyard (Matthew 21:33–46; see Mark 12:1–12).

However, sometimes Jesus introduces images that seem quite new. I think this is the case with what he says about someone, presumably a woman, patching torn cloaks and about someone, presumably a man, pouring new wine into fresh wine skins (Matthew 9:14–17).

Those images seem to originate with Jesus himself. They are things that he has seen men and women doing in their busy lives, taking place around him in ancient Galilee. They are ordinary, everyday activities, and they speak to Jesus of the rule of God that is breaking into our world.

Using the right kind of cloth to mend tears in cloaks and pouring new wine into new wine skins suggest to Jesus how we should react to what is happening as the power of God begins to take hold of our world. New cloth and new wine have come on the scene. We should respond appropriately to the God who is in the business of making all things new (Revelation 21:5).

Let's pray for ourselves that we might share Jesus' vision of where we are in the world and how things around us speak of the coming of God's new kingdom. Through Jesus, an old order is giving way to one that is wonderfully new (Matthew 13:52).

People have different ways of expressing their puzzlement over what happens in their world. 'My life', some say, 'is full of fascinating characters, but I don't seem to be able to work out the plot.' Or they may ask: 'How can I get from here to there?'

What Jesus preaches shows us how he has worked out the plot. A new and final rule of God is taking hold of our world. God's loving power will bring us from here in this life to there in eternal life.

'The kingdom of heaven suffers violence, and the violent bear it away' (Matthew 11:12 own translation). When I read these words, I always think of a wonderful writer called Flannery O'Connor (d.1964). She was only in her twenties when she was diagnosed with lupus. She was expected to live only another five years. But she lived another fourteen.

Before she died, she published many short stories and two novels. One of those novels has the title, *The Violent Bear It Away*. Miss Flannery wrote about violence and pain. Because of the disease from which she suffered, she knew violence and pain in her own body.

She knew too that the kingdom of heaven involves violence, the kind of violence that killed John the Baptist and then Jesus himself. A violent disease caused the death of Miss Flannery before she turned 40.

In *The Violent Bear It Away* and other writings, she shared many wonderful insights about faith. She summed up her own life of faith by saying: 'Grace changes us, and change is painful'. I always remain grateful to Flannery O'Connor for her courageous faith and wonderful writing. I pray for my readers and myself that we may all hear what Miss Flannery said and let it transform our lives. Grace does change us, and change is painful.

NINE

Discerning, Yeast and Treasure

An episode when Jesus was challenged over his disciples picking grain on the Sabbath (Matthew 12:1–8, with a little help from Mark 2:23–28) can guide us when making up our minds on moral matters and reaching a decision. We can draw three principles from this story: healthy tradition, common sense and the presence of Jesus.

First, healthy tradition. Jesus points to a striking example from the past. When they became hungry, King David led his companions into the Temple, where they 'ate the bread of presence', even though it 'was not lawful' for him or the others to do so. Only the priests could eat these 12 loaves brought into the Temple every Sabbath as an offering of thanksgiving (Leviticus 24:3–9). Good examples from the past can guide our decisions. In the case of David and his entourage, a basic human need for food trumped some sacred regulations.

Second, common sense. 'The Sabbath was made for humankind, and not humankind for the Sabbath' (Mark 2:27). Jesus sets himself against a rigid legalism that puts aside ordinary, common sense and seems to imagine that human beings are made for the good of rules and regulations. Such legalism has left behind a long trail of harm. It regularly forgets that regulations are made for the good of human beings, and not vice versa. At times, we need to look over the legal walls to see the real world outside.

Third, we need to remember that we live always in the presence of Jesus, the Lord of the Sabbath. All our discerning and deciding should be directed towards him, whether it happens on the Sabbath or on any other day of the week. He should always be right there in our moments of decision, big or small. Our primary question must be – what does the Lord Jesus want us to do?

'The kingdom of heaven is like yeast that a woman took and mixed in with three measures [= 23 litres] of flour until all of it was leavened' (Matthew 13:33).

From his childhood on, Jesus had innumerable chances of seeing his mother and other women doing just what he said: mixing the right amount of yeast in flour they were kneading ready for putting in the oven. When he saw women doing that kitchen chore, his mind moved ever so easily to God and the kingdom of God that was taking hold of the world. Years later in his preaching Jesus wanted to share with us his experience, and invited us to let prayer arise from seeing for ourselves the power of a little yeast to affect a large batch of dough.

What comes from adding the yeast follows with certainty. The flour will rise, and several fragrant loaves will emerge from the oven. That common, domestic experience entered the way Jesus thought about the powerful, if mysterious, growth of God's reign. The divine power may be hidden but it will certainly leaven everything. Immense, wonderful results are sure to come. We will eat bread together in the kingdom of God.

Among his very short parables, Jesus imagines a man coming across a rich treasure hidden in a field and a merchant looking for precious pearls and finding a uniquely precious pearl (Matthew 13:44–46). When we read these two parables, we might ask ourselves: Who or what is the treasure hidden in the field? Who or what is the uniquely valuable pearl?

Jesus himself is the answer. He is the wonderful treasure. He is the extraordinarily beautiful pearl. Jesus is so marvellous and so valuable that we should be ready to give up everything and let everything else go, because he is the treasure that will remain with us forever. He is the supremely precious pearl that will give us a joy and happiness that no one can ever take from us.

TEN

Little Children and Transfiguration

Jesus knew that children could be peevish and cantankerous (Matthew 11:16, 17). But one can never imagine him behaving like Elisha. When some small boys jeered at that prophet, 'he cursed them in the name of the Lord. Then two she-bears came out of the woods and mauled forty-two of the boys' (2 Kings 2:23, 24). We don't hear that Jeremiah, Ezekiel, and other prophets, down to John the Baptist, behaved in that nasty way with children. Yet they were not remembered as friends of children, let alone their special friends. But Jesus was.

Growing up in Nazareth, Jesus was different from the other young men of his age. He remained unmarried, and had plenty of time to spend with children and show himself to be their special friend.

Jewish society of those days did not particularly value, still less spoil children. The sooner they grew up and started working, the better. Children were down the bottom of the social scale. What did Jesus love and cherish in children?

Children must have appealed to Jesus because they can be amazingly creative and imaginative. They had the imagination to appreciate the stories he told and caught the point of his parables. Children can share a great deal with adults and teach them new ways of seeing things, if adults are open and receptive.

Since they are still very young, children haven't had the time, however, to run up a list of achievements. They have few 'merits' – to use an old-fashioned word. Yes, they can already do much for us adults. But they are normally very happy to receive things; they are glad to be given presents. That makes them role models for entering the kingdom of heaven. As Jesus said, 'unless you change and become like children, you will never enter the kingdom of heaven' (Matthew 18:3).

Ultimately, we don't deserve God's blessings. Compared with God's gifts and God's love for us, our so-called 'merits' are nothing. But we are offered the kingdom of heaven. We should delight in that gift, and be utterly happy to receive God's wonderful and enduring presents. Like little children, we should be supremely happy with what our loving God wants to give us and has already given us.

Matthew clearly wants to juxtapose the transfiguration of Jesus (Matthew 17:1–8) with his crucifixion. The two events are held together by at least six themes, even if those themes may also involve sharp contrasts.

Firstly, two central figures from the Old Testament, Moses and Elijah, join Jesus in the glory of the transfiguration and speak with him. At the crucifixion, Jesus will die in the company of two unnamed criminals crucified on his right hand and left, respectively (Matthew 27:38). Both at the glorious transfiguration and at the shameful crucifixion, two figures share intimately in what happens to Jesus. He is not transfigured alone. He does not die alone.

Second, Matthew notes how in the transfiguration the *clothes* of Jesus became 'radiant as light'. The very garments of Jesus radiated something of his glorious beauty. At Calvary, he was stripped of his clothes (Matthew 27:35) before being crucified in humiliating nakedness.

Third, at the transfiguration the voice of (the invisible) God affirms the identity of Jesus: 'this is my Son, the beloved'. On Calvary, a Roman centurion, who has been in charge of Jesus' execution, confesses the real identity of the criminal he has just put to death as a messianic pretender: 'Truly, this man was God's Son' (Matthew 27:54).

Fourth, the two events provoke awe and even terror. On the mountain of the transfiguration, Peter, James and John 'were overcome with fear'. On Calvary, an earthquake and other signs that accompanied the death of Jesus left the centurion and his squad 'terrified' (Matthew 27:54).

Fifth, followers of Jesus witness both the transfiguration and the crucifixion. Three men – Peter, James and John – who form a core trio within the 12, follow Jesus to a mountain where he is transfigured before their eyes. On Calvary, many women, including Mary Magdalene, Mary the mother of James and Joseph, and the mother of the sons of Zebedee (namely, James and John) watch from a distance at the execution and death of Jesus (Matthew 27:55, 56).

Sixth, at the end of the transfiguration, Peter, James, and John 'looked up [and] saw no one except Jesus' (Matthew 17:8). Matthew refers to Jesus here by his personal name. He does not reach for a title and say, for instance: 'they saw no one but only the Lord'. Matthew anticipates his final, Easter chapter, in which he writes five times of 'Jesus' and never gives him a title, not even that of 'Christ'. 'Jesus' meets Mary Magdalene and her companion as they leave the open and empty tomb. 'Jesus' commissions the eleven disciples to evangelise the whole world.

Matthew clearly wants to juxtapose the transfiguration and crucifixion of Jesus and its aftermath, the resurrection. Those who read his Gospel quickly may link the two events simply on the basis of Elijah being mentioned in both (Matthew 17:3, 4; 27:47, 49). But the links prove to be more complex, fascinating and enriching.

Matthew holds together the transfiguration and crucifixion, because he recognises how suffering and glory are integrated. The Jesus who dies by slow torture on a cross is the Jesus who was transfigured and who will be transfigured in glory.

ELEVEN

A Vineyard, a Bridegroom and a Way of Love

In his parable of the wicked tenants of a vineyard (Matthew 21:33–44), Jesus took up an image from the Old Testament and gave it his own special twist. Isaiah 5:1–7 described a lovely vineyard prepared by God. When it came to vineyards, no one did it better than God. The vineyard was set on a fertile hill; the stones had been cleared away; and a watchtower had been built. The people of Israel themselves were identified with this well-appointed vineyard created by God.

But the vineyard produced only wild grapes. So God let it run down and become overgrown with briars and thorns. The prophet Isaiah pictured a vineyard that started off in wonderful shape but then fell into miserable decay.

The vineyard that Jesus imagined remains perfectly and obviously productive. There is never anything wrong with the vineyard he spoke about. The problem is with the wicked tenants, who become serial killers. They mistreat and murder some of the agents sent to them by the rich and powerful owner of the vineyard.

Then they commit their supreme crime when they kill the owner's son.

But the tenants have no chance of getting away with murdering the young man, seizing the vineyard, and making it their own property. They are out of their minds when they deal that way with the owner and those he sends to them. He will come quickly with an armed force, execute the murderers, and put his choice vineyard into the hands of other tenants.

It's all a sad picture of us human beings. Our thinking is totally astray and not in touch with reality, if we fail to deal with God as we should. We are not going to get away with it, if we resist and reject God, the God from whom we come, the God who has given us everything, the God to whom we are going. It is simply irrational not to deal with God as we should.

Yet, finally, love rather than reason will straighten us out and help us relate appropriately to the loving God to whom we owe everything. In the parable, the wicked tenants show no love but only reason gone seriously wrong. Let us ask our loving God to fill us with the kind of love that will help us to think straight and live the way we should.

This story preached by Jesus is the only parable in which he himself clearly appears. He is obviously the son, or, as he is called in Mark's version of the parable, the 'one beloved son' (Mark 12:6). We might remember here what God said at the transfiguration of Jesus: 'this is my beloved Son. Listen to him.' This is the only parable in which Jesus the Son of God enjoys, so to speak, a walk-on part.

Rejecting Jesus has no future. It means doing something that in the long term or even in the short term will prove self-destructive. On the surface the parable carries a negative message. To forget that we are tenants for God, even to the point of rejecting Jesus, is an insane policy. But we can transpose all this into a positive message. Behaving as God's loyal servants and faithful tenants, listening to Jesus, and following him will bring nothing but life and life in abundance. It will mean living forever in a marvellous, productive vineyard, a kind of heavenly Tuscany or Provence.

The story of the five wise and the five foolish bridesmaids leaves us with several puzzles (Matthew 25:1–13). Why does the bridegroom turn up so late in the night? When the foolish bridesmaids head off at midnight to buy oil for their lamps, who is going to sell it to them? Are we meant to think of some ancient store providing service into the early hours of the morning? How are we to understand the words with which the parable ends: 'Keep awake . . . for you know neither the day nor the hour'? After all, the wise bridesmaids also fall asleep. None of the ten young women stays awake.

But what is the heart of the story? I think it is a picture of us all waiting for Christ the bridegroom, the beautiful bridegroom who we can fall in love with forever. The parable suggests what the saintly Fr Pedro Arrupe, a deceased superior general of the Jesuits, used to say: 'Fall in love with Jesus. Stay in love with Jesus. And everything will take care of itself.'

Jesus is the radiantly beautiful bridegroom with whom we can fall in love. He is the bridegroom for whom we should always stay awake, the bridegroom whom we should love, serve, and wait for all the days of our lives.

In one of his famous books, *Civilization and its Discontents*, Sigmund Freud quoted what he called the 'grandiose' commandment, 'You shall love your neighbour as yourself.' Freud then asked: 'Why should I do this? How can it be possible?' Freud continued: 'If I am to love someone, he must in some way deserve it. But so many men don't.' He added that if the commandment stated 'love your neighbour as your neighbour loves you', he would take no exception to it. But, as the love commandment stood, Freud found it unreasonable and, in fact, impossible to fulfil.

Freud was objecting to what he read in Leviticus 19:18. Growing up in a Jewish family, he knew that text: 'You shall love your neighbour as yourself.' Jesus also grew up in a Jewish family. He also knew that text. So, far from rejecting it, he did two startling things with it, things no one had ever done before.

Firstly, Jesus joined the command to love our neighbour with the command to love our God (Matthew 22:34–40). We cannot talk sincerely about loving God unless we practise love towards our neighbour. Second, as far as Jesus was concerned, our neighbour is not merely any man or woman who deserves our love but simply any man or woman – above all, anyone whatsoever in serious need or distress.

In another passage from Matthew, Jesus gives us examples of such people who desperately need help: the sick, those who are hungry and have no jobs to put clothes on their back or food on their table, those in prison and strangers with nowhere to live (Matthew 25:31–46). The list is open-ended. We can easily add others who suffer: 'I belonged to an ethnic majority and you reached out to me in friendship. I was uneducated and you spent years teaching me. I was on parole from jail, and you helped me get a job.'

In one sense, Freud was right. What Jesus asks for can seem unreasonable, and left to ourselves it is very hard to fulfil. But with his help we can put love into action.

When I studied at the University of Cambridge, I met a remarkable couple from South Africa, Jimmy S. and his wife. If homeless tramps knocked at their door, they would invite them to come in, sit down and share a meal. Many of my readers will know people like Jimmy and his wife. Grace let them accept Jesus' 'unreasonable' call to love and put that love into practice. We can only pray: 'Jesus, help us, help me, to hear and put your love into action.'

TWELVE

'I am with you always'

Matthew 28:20

A few years ago a young friend of mine was ordained a priest in Vietnam. When he came back to Melbourne to finish his studies, I asked him whether he had many letters or emails to answer. 'No,' he said, 'my relatives, friends, and supporters did not write. They all came to be present at the ordination and my first Mass.'

Of course, coming yourself is the best present of all. That's the finest way of showing your love and support for someone. And that's just what the Son of God did. He didn't merely send us messages. But he came himself in person – 'Emmanuel' or 'God is with us' (Matthew 1:23). That's how much the Son of God cared for us and loved us. But then he did something that the friends of that young Vietnamese priest could not do. 'God-with-us' promised to be with us always.

The Gospel of Matthew ends with Jesus now risen from the dead and promising to remain with his followers forever. But how does this presence express itself? What forms does it take?

For centuries, Catholics and some other Christians regularly spoke of Christ's presence in the Eucharist as 'the real presence'. It was a way of recognising that, while Christ is present in many other ways, his personal presence in the Blessed Sacrament is the supreme and most precious form of his presence.

However, the expression could be misunderstood in two ways. First, the unwary might take it to imply that the other forms of Christ's presence – let us say, his presence in all those human beings who are sick, hungry, imprisoned, homeless, and suffering other misfortunes – is not 'real' but only imaginary. Yes, the presence of Christ differs. But his presence is always real, never imaginary.

Second, talk of 'real presence' might suggest that there is also a 'real absence' of Christ. This would be to forget that Christ is never and nowhere absent. There is no place where we are distant and separated from him. For each of us, he is the constant, loving Friend who accompanies us, in good times and bad times, right through our lives.

In its 1963 Constitution on the Divine Liturgy, *Sacrosanctum Concilium*, the Second Vatican Council spelled out five forms of Christ's presence (no. 7). They can bring to life the promise with which the Gospel of Matthew ends.

Firstly, Christ is present wherever and whenever the members of his Church gather to pray and sing together. As he promised, ' . . . where two or three are gathered in my name, I am there among them' (Matthew 18:20).

So, far from remaining a mere crowd of individuals, the assembled community displays the presence of the risen Christ.

Second, Christ also becomes present 'in his word, since it is he himself who speaks when the holy Scriptures are read in church'. This teaching from Vatican II challenges all those who read in church to do so with dignity, clarity, and devotion. Through the words they proclaim, they bring to others the powerful presence of the risen Lord. The texts they announce are inspired, and should be inspiring.

Third, Christ is potently present, when we celebrate any of the sacraments. The passage from Vatican II quotes what St Augustine said of baptism: 'when anyone baptises, it is Christ himself who baptises'. He is the real, even if invisible, minister of all the sacraments. We see and hear the visible ministers of the sacraments: the ordained priests who administer the sacrament of reconciliation to those who confess their sins, or the married couples who give each other the grace of matrimony through their bodily and personal union. But, invisibly and really, it is the risen Lord who is present to heal sinners and reconcile them with God and the community. Christ is the one who ministers the sacrament of matrimony to husband and wife and remains always there to help them grow in mutual love.

Fourth, the risen Christ is present, Vatican II teaches, 'in the person' of his ministers at the Eucharist. When celebrating the Eucharist, ordained priests are visible signs of the invisible but dynamically present Christ. At every Eucharist, Christ is the Offerer, the One who continues to offer, invisibly yet truly, the self-sacrifice he offered once and for all at the end of his earthly life – in his passion, death, and resurrection. He takes up into this offering the visible priest and the assembled faithful. The ordained priests act 'in the person of Christ', but not in the sense of replacing him or substituting for him. They act as visible signs of his invisible and powerful presence as *the* Offerer and *the* Offering.

Fifth, Vatican II speaks of Christ being present 'supremely' in the consecrated, Eucharistic elements of bread and wine. His presence in the Eucharist is the most marvellous and intense presence among us. His 'being there' for us, under the appearances of bread and wine, looks extraordinarily simple. But it is something only God can bring about. When Jesus took some bread and wine and changed them into his body and blood, he made himself vividly present not only then but also at every Eucharist that will be celebrated until the end of time. Through the Eucharist he gives himself to be our food as we move through life into eternity.

These then are five ways in which Vatican II spoke of the presence of the risen Christ whenever we celebrate any form of the liturgy. His liturgical presence reaches its highest point in the celebration of the Eucharist and the consecrated Eucharistic elements. But his presence is not limited to the liturgy.

Three years after Vatican II ended, Pope Paul VI visited Bogotá (Colombia) for the International Eucharistic Congress of 1968. When speaking to farm workers, he linked the presence of Christ in the Eucharist with his presence in all who are homeless, hungry, sick, imprisoned, exiled, and suffering in other ways. Christ is present in all human pain and in every human being who suffers – especially in those who face terrible need and distress.

Paul VI treasured the supreme presence of Christ in the Eucharist. It made him recognise a further form of Christ's presence – in those who worked and suffered in the dangerous countryside of Colombia.

A few years later at his Holy Thursday homily in the cathedral of Brisbane (Australia), Archbishop Frank Rush honoured the wonderful gift of the Eucharist, 'the source of all the Church's strength' and 'the food for our journey through life'. The Eucharistic presence made him recall in the same homily how 'every day Christ's passion continues in his people'. He added very specifically, 'Over at St Vincent's Hostel for Homeless People in South Brisbane, they will give beds tonight to about 180 men. Of these, about sixty will be between the ages of 16 and 25. Today they will have fed 1,400 men and women who otherwise would not have eaten a decent meal.'

Paul VI and Archbishop Rush, like Mother Teresa of Calcutta and countless other men and women down the centuries, acknowledged the essential bond between worshipping Christ present in the Eucharist and serving him in the suffering. Those who suffer also embody his presence. When we receive Christ present in the Eucharist, we are called to recognise his presence in all those men and women who are in pain and desperately need our help.

The risen Christ committed himself to be with us always. We find that presence, promised at the end of Matthew's Gospel, not only when we gather to pray but also when we move out to serve those in distress.

MARK'S GOSPEL

THIRTEEN

In Praise of Mark

The Gospel of Mark has exercised a profound influence on my spiritual life – in particular, through three themes that shape the whole story: the revelation of Jesus' personal identity; the call to follow him on the way of the cross; and the figure of Peter.

Firstly, Mark opens by announcing 'the beginning of the good news of Jesus Christ, the Son of God' (1:1). A few verses later, at the baptism of Jesus, a voice from heaven addresses him: 'You are my Son, the Beloved; with you I am well pleased.' Right at the outset, the writer of the Gospel and then God make clear the divine identity of Jesus.

The invisible demonic forces, who take possession of people, show at once that they know with whom they are dealing. In the synagogue of Capernaum, an unclean spirit speaks in their name: 'What have you to do with us, Jesus of Nazareth? Have you come to destroy us? I know who you are, the Holy One of God' (1:24; see 5:7).

But no human being who meets Jesus succeeds in grasping his *full* identity. Peter acknowledges Jesus to be the anointed deliverer sent by God: 'You are the Christ' (8:29). Then, with James and John on the mountain of the transfiguration, Peter hears God speaking from a cloud: 'This is my Son, the Beloved; listen to him' (9:7). When Jesus enters Jerusalem, a crowd of people gather and acclaim Jesus as the anointed Son of David. He victoriously moves into the city like a peasant king riding on a donkey (11:1–11). Yet so far neither Peter nor anyone else breaks through to the great secret at the heart of Jesus' personal existence.

It is only when Jesus utters a loud cry and dies on the cross that for the first time in Mark's Gospel a human being grasps his divine identity. The Roman centurion in charge of Jesus' execution, seeing how he has breathed his last, declares: 'Truly this man was a Son of God' (15:39). It is an outsider, used to brutal work in the emperor's service including crucifying an innocent man, who first breaks through the divine incognito and acknowledges the mysterious identity at the heart of Jesus' existence.

The confession of the centurion has always challenged me to be ready to recognise the Lord even (or especially) in grim and painful moments of life. The Son is always there in dark times, even when we face agonising suffering that may almost seem as absurd and humiliating as a crucifixion. Such disturbing episodes can become privileged occasions that eloquently reveal to us the presence of Jesus, the divine Son of God who has suffered with us and for us.

Second, in Mark's Gospel, Jesus heals many people and even brings one dead person back to life, the daughter of Jairus (5:22–43). The healing of Bartimaeus (10:46–52), however, is truly unique. He is the only case of someone healed by Jesus who then becomes his follower. This blind man regains his sight and 'follows Jesus on the way'.

No one else in this Gospel does just that. Many others are cured by Jesus, and presumably do all kinds of good things afterwards. But we never read of any of these people becoming followers of Jesus, let alone deciding then and there to become a disciple and take to the road with Jesus.

Yes, it's a unique case, that of Bartimaeus. But let's not miss where it takes place and where Bartimaeus' healing leads him. Regaining his sight by the roadside in Jericho, he begins to follow Jesus 'on the way' leading up to Jerusalem, the place where Jesus will soon be put to death and raised from the dead. Bartimaeus joins Jesus on the way of the cross, the road to Calvary and resurrection.

Mark uses the blind beggar to say to his readers, 'If you are going to follow Jesus on the way of the cross, you too must have your eyes opened. The Lord must give you spiritual sight if you are to walk faithfully with your Master to the place of crucifixion and resurrection.'

Mark wrote his Gospel at the time of severe persecution. He had his message for a persecuted Church and for all of us. Our eyes need to be opened and our hearts changed, if we are to follow Jesus to Calvary and beyond.

Like Bartimaeus, we too must pray and do so constantly: 'Jesus, Son of David, have mercy on us'.

Third, I treasure Mark's Gospel for allowing us to hear the testimony of St Peter. An ancient tradition attributed this Gospel to John Mark (mentioned in Acts 12:12 and 15:37, Philemon 24) and pictured him as writing down the preaching of Peter (see 1 Peter 5:13). Many modern scholars have cast doubt on this tradition. But in a detailed study, *Jesus and the Eyewitnesses: The Gospels as Eyewitness Testimony* (Grand Rapids, Mich.: Eerdmans, 2006), Richard Bauckham has argued convincingly that Mark's Gospel derives from the eyewitness testimony of Peter. Bauckham produces persuasive evidence to reinstate the case of Simon Peter being the major source for the Gospel of Mark.

Peter holds the Gospel together, being named at the beginning (1:16–18) and then right through to the end (16:7). Readers can share the eyewitness perspective that the testimony of Peter embodied, and come to appreciate how much he had to learn 'on the job' as leader of the 12.

Here the most poignant example concerns the passion and death of Jesus. Peter has spoken for himself and the others: 'We have left everything and followed you' (10:28). But only a few chapters later, when Jesus is arrested in the Garden of Gethsemane, Peter and the other disciples leave everything to get away from Jesus – a flight symbolised by the mysterious young man who evades arrest by leaving his garment behind and fleeing naked into the night (14:50–52).

Peter uses very strong language to deny that he even knows Jesus and even swears that on oath (14:66–72). He is rehabilitated when Jesus appears to him (16:7), and enables him to translate the trauma of failure into a lifetime of faithful service crowned with a martyr's death.

I have learned much from the Gospel of Mark to guide me along the road of life, particularly through the stories of the centurion, Bartimaeus and Peter. I hope and pray that others may share my experience.

FOURTEEN

Serving, Healing, Life-giving and Robbing

The Gospel of Mark uses a significant verb four times: twice at the beginning, once at the halfway mark, and once at the end. It's the verb 'to serve' – in Greek *diakonein*, linked to the noun 'deacon'.

At the start, we read of Jesus spending 40 days in the wilderness 'with the wild beasts' but with 'the angels serving him' (Mark 1:13 own translation). Shortly after that, Jesus began preaching, calling his disciples, and working miracles. Early in this ministry, he visited the home of Simon Peter and found Peter's mother-in-law in bed and suffering from a high fever. Jesus took her by the hand and the fever left her. She got up and 'began serving' him, as well as the others present. He didn't stop her from doing that by suggesting: 'take it easy for a while; you have just been seriously ill'.

Halfway through the story which Mark tells, Jesus reminded his male disciples who were anxious for power and privilege that 'the Son of Man came not to be served but to serve' (Mark 10:45). Yet he did not forbid many women, like Mary Magdalene, who travelled in his entourage, from 'serving him'. Those women even went to the place of execution on Calvary and remained courageously present when Jesus was crucified (Mark 15:40, 41).

Jesus did not merely say, 'the Son of Man has come to serve'. He lived that way – right through to his crucifixion. Jesus showed himself to be the servant of all, the One who in life and death constantly served others. But serving others also meant *allowing others to serve him*. He let angels, Peter's mother-in-law, Mary Magdalene, and many other women be his servants.

The Gospel of Mark names three of the 'many' women who 'served' Jesus in Galilee and followed him right through to his death on the cross: Mary Magdalene, Mary the mother of James and Joses (see Mark 6:3), and Salome (Mark 15:40, 41). These three women belonged to a large group, and I like to think that, without being named, Peter's mother-in-law was one of the group. In Galilee, she was cured by Jesus and began to serve him. She could well have been one of the courageous women who followed him to Jerusalem and stood there on Calvary at his passing from this world – serving him through to the end.

It's not simply a matter of an either/or: either serving or being served. Part of serving others involves allowing them to serve us. Jesus was truly our suffering servant, who in life and in death proved himself the servant of all. But being our servant also meant allowing others to serve him. The way Mark deploys the verb 'to serve' makes that abundantly clear.

Peter's mother-in-law is one of those minor characters in the Gospel stories whom I hope to meet in the next life. Since last year she has started coming into my prayer. I find myself sitting in a warm, early evening on a hillside near the Sea of Galilee, with a lovely breeze coming off the water. Further up the hill Jesus is talking with Peter, Andrew, James, and John. After a long day of preaching, they are all sharing a cup of wine with Jesus, and I am looking up at the five of them.

Then Peter's mother-in-law suddenly turns up, gives me a cup of wine, and says: 'have a drink and just wait here until the Master comes down to bless you'. It's the kind of thing you might expect from her. When she was cured by Jesus, she straightaway began to serve him and others with food and drink. Prayer has allowed me to know and admire her love for Jesus. I am grateful for the way she turns up in prayer and gives me some wine to drink.

Mark 1:40-45 pictures a meeting between Jesus and a man suffering from leprosy. To suffer from leprosy in those days was a death sentence. Lepers were feared and avoided. They were isolated and could not live in normal society. Their contagious disease put them under a death sentence, both physically and socially. In Mark's story, a leper went in search of Jesus as his last chance and only hope.

The leper simply said to Jesus: 'Lord, if you choose, you can make me clean.' He put total trust in the power of Jesus – in the power of what Jesus might say in reply. Jesus wanted to cure him, but did not say at once: 'I do so choose; be made clean.' First he stretched out his hand and touched the leper, evidently laying a hand on a face ravaged by leprosy. Jesus was not content to love the leper and cure him, so to speak, from a distance. He wanted to have real, physical contact with the poor man before he healed him. It was only after he touched the leper that he cured him.

Each of us has something serious that we suffer from. Whatever it is, Jesus cares for us in our sufferings. But he is not content to remain at a distance from us, simply doing things *for us* and saying things *to us*. He wants to have real contact *with us*. Jesus stretches out his hand and touches each of us. He comes into contact with us and touches us, above all when he comes into us through Holy Communion. He does this, because he loves us through and through.

These days I have been thinking and writing about love. This has meant examining how love is inherently relational, oriented towards others, committed to others, and taking responsibility for others. That's just what we find in Mark's story. Jesus is utterly oriented towards the leper; he is totally committed to him, and takes responsibility for him. The love of Jesus is nothing if not inherently relational.

To be sure, the word 'love' does not turn up explicitly in Mark's account of Jesus healing the leper. But the story does say that when Jesus met the leper, 'his heart went out to him' (Mark 1:41). That's the best way of translating the wonderful word in the original (Greek) text: *splanchnistheis*. Some translations weaken the force of what Mark wrote: 'he felt sorry for him', or 'he had compassion for him', or 'he felt pity for him'. We capture the meaning best by saying, 'his heart went out to him'. As we might say, Jesus experienced a gut reaction of love.

Finally, the cleansing of the leper offers a chance of reflecting on the lepers of today. At the time of Jesus, leprosy was considered so contagious that lepers were quarantined for life. They were forced to live apart from the rest of the community. They had no one to care for them, except other lepers. Modern society does not lack lepers: physical lepers like those suffering from HIV/AIDS; psychological lepers like those with mental illness or disabilities; moral lepers like those who have perpetrated horrible crimes; economic lepers like those who never find employment; and the rest. Jesus is always their special friend. He reaches out to touch them and help them. He wants us to do the same – to care for them and be their friend.

Healing a man with a withered hand (Mark 3:1-6) belongs among the early miracles worked by Jesus. It differs from some of the earlier cures: for instance the cleansing of a leper (Mark 1:40–45) and the healing of a paralytic (Mark 2:1–12).

Compared with those stories, healing the hand of an anonymous man may seem a minor affair. Unlike the leper, he was not excluded from ordinary society or from attending religious services. Unlike the paralytic, he was not carried around in a litter, but could walk on his own two feet and enter a synagogue to worship with others on the Sabbath.

But the healing of the man with a withered hand has its own precious feature, a question Jesus put to his dangerous critics: 'Is it lawful to do good or to do harm on the Sabbath, to save life or to kill?' Then with a word of command, he healed the man. The immediate impact was lethal. Some understood such a cure to offend against the prohibition of work on the Sabbath. They left the synagogue and starting plotting to do away with Jesus – the first time in Mark's Gospel that we hear of people joining forces to plan the death of Jesus (Mark 3:6). A small miracle becomes the occasion of a deadly threat to Jesus.

The miracle also becomes the occasion for Jesus himself to say what he is about: doing good and saving life. It reveals his desire to do good and save lives at any cost – even at the cost of his own life. Jesus is more concerned with restoring a human being to full health than obeying the prohibition of work on the Sabbath. He 'saves life', even at the clear risk of losing his own.

Human history has seen two main ways of practising robbery: by being burglars or bandits. We can rob others by breaking into their house secretly and stealing their goods. Or else we can confront the occupants with guns or knives, lock them up, and plunder their possessions.

Both kinds of robbers are used to describe what Jesus is about. He will come unexpectedly like a thief in the night (Matthew 24:43; 1 Thessalonians 5:2; Revelation 3:3). He likens himself to a 'bandit' who breaks into the house of a strong, well-armed man, ties him up and proceeds to rob him of his possessions (Mark 3:27).

Remembering the two vivid and unusual images of Jesus, we might pray: 'Jesus, thief in the night, let us be ready for your coming. Jesus, powerful bandit, let us trust that you are more powerful than all the forces of evil.'

FIFTEEN

Seed, Growth and a Storm

'Some seed fell on the path, and the birds came and ate it up ... These are the ones on the path where the word is sown: when they hear, Satan immediately comes and takes away the word that is sown in them' (Mark 4:4, 15).

When we read these two verses, we might have some objections to both the image and its application. Let me explain.

Firstly, the image. Birds come and eat seed not only from the edge of paths but also from wherever they can find it. A year ago, workmen dug a trench to lay some pipes across the back lawn of the college where I live. After installing the pipes and filling up the trench, they sprinkled some seed over the new soil. Doves and other birds arrived instantly. It wasn't at the edge of the path but right across the middle of the lawn that the birds were having a feast day. They ate up seed wherever they could find it.

And then what about associating birds with Satan, who comes and carries off the word of God? Apart from such birds as ugly crows who seem like the vermin of the air, it seems a bit tough on such birds that turn up on my back lawn – blackbirds, cockatoos, doves, galahs, ground parrots, lorikeets, magpies, mudlarks, a few kookaburras and the rest – to picture them as stand-ins for Satan. But one gets the point. It's not enough to hear the word of God in a merely superficial way, which does not allow it to sink into our minds and hearts.

Nowadays this explanation of the parable of the sower seems more important than ever. We are bombarded with endless messages – on our TV and computer screens, through the radio and newspapers, and on the mobile phones and iPads that hardly leave our hands. So many words come at us in this world of hyper-information. We need to be very discerning and willing to stop and listen carefully, if we are to hear the word addressed to us by God. We can only pray: 'Holy Spirit, we are bombarded with so much noise. Help us to hear the word of God, to take it in, and quietly treasure it as seed for our true lives.'

In a few months, at the back of my college, roses will bud and come into flower. An oak tree will soon look gloriously green again. In the vegetable garden, lettuce, onions and beans will flourish. Spring growth will soon be on the way.

Most of us have no idea of how all that growth happens. But it does happen, and there's no stopping it (Mark 4:26–29). Jesus did not speak, of course, about roses, oak trees, and vegetables, but about the seed of wheat or barley that a farmer sows in a field. Given the right conditions, that seed will germinate, sprout, and grow right through to harvest time. Jesus wanted to share with us his deep trust in the power of God's kingdom. Growth is in the air; the harvest is on the way.

Mysteriously, but powerfully, the life and growth of God's kingdom surrounds us. Let us come with joy into the presence of the Lord, the Lord who gives us growth and life, right through to the final harvest.

Jesus, thank God, was no systematic theologian. He said many challenging things, but he never tried to bring them all into synthesis. He would stress one side of the picture, and then the other side of the picture. But he never wanted to bring the two sides into a convincing synthesis.

Let me take one example of Jesus' practice, his parable of the sower and the seed (Mark 4:1–9). By speaking of rocky ground, good soil, and the rest, Jesus highlighted our receiving or not receiving the seed. That parable emphasised different outcomes that arise from the different ways the seed or word of God is received or not received.

In a further parable (Mark 4:26–29), he spoke of seed sprouting and growing energetically. All the soil seems to be equally good, and the results of the seed being sown will come along infallibly. God and the word of God are at work. The initiative of God will have its way.

I remain very grateful that Jesus has left us these two stories. They fill each other out. On the one hand, we need to check ourselves. Are we good soil that receives openly and generously the word of God? On the other hand, we need to reverence the mysteriously powerful way in which God works in our lives. Like the farmer in the second parable, we go to bed in the evening; we sleep, we wake in the morning, and we rise to face another day. Right through our sleeping and our waking hours, God remains always at work, bringing about at all times what God knows to be best for ourselves and for others.

Ever since he was elected in March 2013, the media and the internet have spread stories about Pope Francis and the way he reaches out to help people. My favourite story concerns a 35-year-old woman in Rome. Anna found out that she was pregnant. The man she was having an affair with told her that he would not take responsibility for the child. He was married. It was too embarrassing. He urged her to have an abortion.

Anna felt desperate and full of fear. In her misery she wrote a letter to Pope Francis. To her astonishment, he phoned her a few days later. 'Don't let anyone push you around,' he told her. 'Have the baby, and if you can't find a priest to baptise the baby, I'll do it myself.' Anna promised the Pope that if the baby was a boy, she would call him Francesco. I'm only sorry that she didn't also promise him that, if the baby was a girl, she would call her Francesca.

From time to time, we all meet people like Anna, people who find themselves caught in a storm (Mark 4:35-41) and without hope about getting out alive. Sometimes, thank God, we have been in a position to calm their fears and help them find a way ahead.

At other times we can feel up against it ourselves. At sea and with waves breaking over us, we seem to be going down. Things have become very fearful, and the Lord doesn't seem to be doing anything for us.

But the Lord is always present and there to save us. Every one of us is infinitely dear to him. He cares for us far more than we could ever care for ourselves. In the words of a modern hymn, 'Do not be afraid. I am with you. I have called you by your name; you are mine. I have called you by your name; you are mine.'

SIXTEEN

Two Women, Two Conversations and Hard Hearts

One passage in Mark's Gospel tells the story of two women being healed by Jesus: one a grown woman who has suffered from constant bleeding for 12 years and the other a girl who falls ill and dies (Mark 5:22–43).

Because of her bleeding, the woman was regarded by Jewish law as permanently unclean. She was socially and religiously marginalised, an outcast shunned by her community, an embarrassment to her family, and not in a condition to get married to some man. In a word, she was socially and religiously dead. The little girl suffered a physical death. Seemingly forever, she was cut off from her family and friends when she fell ill and then passed away. For both women, Jesus came on the scene and radically changed a deadly situation for each of them.

By curing her haemorrhage, Jesus brought the woman back from her social and religious death. He then brought the young girl back to her family and friends by raising her from the dead.

Mark gives us the name of the girl's father, Jairus, but does not name either the girl or the woman. In the story, both of them remain anonymous. Yet their lives have been rescued from silence and anonymity. Around the world, year by passing year, those who share in the Eucharist hear about these two women. They are remembered and cherished because on a certain day they both met Jesus, one after the other, and their stories were changed forever.

One of them met Jesus because she went looking for him and touched his cloak. The other was far too sick to leave her bed. Her father went looking for Jesus, and Jesus came to her. It does not matter very much how the two women encountered Jesus. What matters is that they did meet him. Meeting him changed their lives for all time.

Few women who read or hear the passage from Mark suffer, like the first woman in his story, from permanent menstrual bleeding. None of those who read or hear the passage will have died and lie stretched out dead like the 12-year-old girl. But in other ways all of us, both women and men, are ill and desperately need Jesus and his healing, life-giving touch. He is always there to heal our sick and deadly situations and to change our lives forever.

It does not matter how we meet Jesus. What matters is that we do meet him, and that this can happen day by day. Meeting him regularly will transform our existence. Jesus is always there for us – to heal us and save us constantly from all forms of death that afflict us. He is nothing less than our true healer and constant friend.

In the Gospel of Mark, we find women talking to each other only on two occasions. Both occasions involve life and death, but in remarkably different ways.

The first occasion arises when Herod Antipas invites many rich and influential people to an evening banquet (Mark 6:21–29). Salome, the daughter of Herodias, dances for the king and his guests. Herod is so pleased with the girl's performance that he promises to give her anything she asks for. Salome goes off and says to her mother, 'What should I ask for?' Herodias replies, 'The head of John the Baptist'.

Only a brief conversation takes place when the two women, Salome and her mother Herodias, meet and talk together. The result is that Salome takes a horribly tragic request to the king: she wants the head of John the Baptist on a dish. This is the first occasion in Mark's Gospel when we come across two women talking together.

The second occasion turns up much later in the Gospel, right in the final chapter. On the first Easter Sunday morning, three women, Mary Magdalene, Mary the mother of James, and Salome go to the tomb where Jesus had been hastily buried. They bring spices to anoint the body and complete the burial. On the way to the grave, they anxiously ask each other: 'Who will roll away the stone for us from the entrance to the tomb?' (Mark 16:3). To their utter astonishment, they discover the tomb to be open and empty. They hear the message of an angel: 'He has been raised; he is not here. Look, there is the place they laid him' (Mark 16:6).

When the three women talk to each other early on the first Easter Sunday morning, it's all very different from what we read in Chapter 6 of Mark's Gospel. There, Herodias and her daughter speak with each other late one dark evening, when light had gone out of the sky. Under cover of night and driven by hatred, they plot and bring about the violent death of John the Baptist. In the darkness, their conversation leads to a saintly prisoner being beheaded in a dungeon. But when Mary Magdalene and her women companions talk with each other one spring morning, they suddenly find themselves confronted with a unique message of life, the resurrection and the glorious, new existence of Jesus, the Master whom they love dearly.

These three holy women remind us of the dramatic choice we all face: between death and life. King Herod, his wife Herodias, and her daughter Salome represent what wicked and powerful people may offer us: only the darkness of night and death. Mary Magdalene and her two friends symbolise something totally different. As the light of a wonderful spring morning floods into the sky, they point us to life, glorious new life here and hereafter.

'Do you still not perceive or understand? Are your hearts hardened? Do you have eyes and fail to see? Do you have ears, and fail to hear? . . . Do you not yet understand?' (Mark 8:17, 18, 21).

Jesus directs these hard words to his disciples, or rather to a core group of his followers in a boat with him. A few chapters earlier, Jesus has said more or less the same when talking about 'those outside' (Mark 4:12), those to whom he has spoken in parables but are not his followers. Now he reproaches his close followers, those who have been privileged witnesses in his ministry. They have seen physically what he has done. But they don't understand what it means. They have heard physically what he says. But they don't grasp what his words signify. All of this has happened – or rather has failed to happen – because their hearts are hardened.

It is in parables that Jesus has been speaking to his followers. Parables are questions that wait for an answer. In life-changing ways, they reveal what is happening in our world. But no one is deafer than those who are unwilling to hear. No one is more blind than those who deliberately look away.

Let us pray that Jesus will open our eyes and help us to see what he is doing in our lives. Let us pray that he will change our hearts and help us to hear what he is saying to us in so many ways.

SEVENTEEN

The Transfiguration, Being Widowed and the Passion

In the Bible and in Christian history, mountains have been special places for experiencing God. Moses encountered God at a burning bush near Mt Horeb. This encounter with God prefigured the experiences of God that came to the people of Israel at Mt Sinai. Mountains rise high above the ordinary business of human life and lift us up towards the realm of God.

In Mark's Gospel, at his baptism in the River Jordan, Jesus is the one who hears a heavenly voice saying: 'You are my Son, the Beloved; with you I am well pleased' (Mark 1:11). On the mountain of the transfiguration, it is the three disciples who hear a voice from out of a cloud: 'This is my Son, the Beloved; listen to him' (Mark 9:7).

Even more than Western Christians, Eastern Christians treasure the story of the transfiguration, the story of how three of Jesus' disciples glimpsed a unique beauty shining forth from him. They saw the beauty of God on the face of Jesus.

Eastern Christians know what the transfiguration does for us. In their icons they express the beauty of God on the face of Christ, that beauty which shone on the mount of transfiguration and changed for ever the lives of the three disciples.

The classical Russian novelist, Dostoevsky, wrote in a letter to his niece, 'There is only one perfectly beautiful person: Christ.' In the next novel that he wrote (*The Idiot*), Dostoevsky said, 'It is beauty that will save the world.' He shared with other Eastern Christians a rich sense of the beauty of Christ, that unique beauty that shone forth on the mount of transfiguration and can change our lives forever.

In 2015, we celebrated 500 years since the birth of a great Western mystic, Teresa of Avila. Many painters and sculptors have been drawn to depict St Teresa. Gian Lorenzo Bernini (d. 1680) left us an extraordinary statue of Teresa in ecstasy, a statue in which her beauty reflects the beauty of the One she loved so much, the radiantly beautiful Jesus. Bernini's work does not include Jesus himself but only his messenger, a glorious angel piercing the heart of Teresa with a dart of love. The angel is a kind of double for Jesus. The radiantly beautiful angel expresses the radiantly beautiful Jesus and his beauty that transfigured Teresa herself.

That's ultimately what the transfiguration is about. Jesus himself is transformed and that means the transformation of his disciples. His beauty shines forth, and that beauty transforms those who catch even a glimpse of it.

May all of us glimpse his beauty and let it transform our lives. Then, like the disciples, we will look around and see no one with us anymore but only Jesus (Mark 9:8). He will fill our lives, once his beauty has filled our hearts.

In November 2015, Michelle Payne made history by being the first woman to ride the winner of the Melbourne Cup, the classic Australian horse race that comes in early November each year – 'the race that stops the nation'. The public cheered Michelle, her brother Steve, the strapper who got the horse into shape for the big race, and the whole Payne family. What some may not have known, however, was that her father lost his wife in a traffic accident; he went ahead and raised their ten children himself. He was a role model for widowers and showed what they can achieve despite the difficulties.

The Bible has more to say about courageous widows, women who lost their husbands but pushed ahead with life. One widow in the town of Sidon, through a time of terrible famine, generously looked after the prophet Elijah (1 Kings 17:10–16). The story of this widow with her young son is linked in the liturgy (thirty-second Sunday of the year, cycle B) with a widow in Jerusalem (Mark 12:41–44).

One day in the Temple precinct, Jesus watched some well-off people making big contributions. Then he caught sight of a widow, a very poor widow making a tiny offering for the upkeep of the Temple: two small coins, the equivalent of a penny.

We don't know the name of the widow or anything about her life and her dead husband. But I can write of her today, because of the marvellous thing Jesus said about her: 'This poor widow has put in more than all those who are contributing to the treasury. For all of them have contributed out of their abundance; but she out of her poverty has put in everything she had, all she had to live on.'

Jesus didn't blame the well-off people who made big contributions out of their surplus wealth. Rather he praised the utterly poor widow who was willing to give God everything she owned. That was a stunning act of generosity on the part of a completely indigent person.

The Old Testament Scriptures often mention widows and orphans as those whom God cares about in a special way. These vulnerable people lack the normal social supports and need special help from other human beings. In the case of Michelle Payne's family, it was a matter of a widower and ten orphaned children.

What comes through loud and clear from those passages in 1 Kings 17 and Mark 12 is the generosity of widows: the generosity of the widow who cared for the prophet Elijah and the generosity of the widow in Jerusalem who made her contribution to keep the worship of God going in the Temple.

You might say that the widow in Sidon practised in a special way love for her neighbour. To be sure, Elijah was a quite extraordinary neighbour. But he still was another human being in need of help. For three years the widow gave him the food and lodging that he needed. The widow whom Jesus singled out for praise when making her donation in the Temple was honouring God and expressing her love for God. She gave the little she had to support the divine service.

The first widow reached out 'horizontally' to another human being in his basic needs. The second widow reached out 'vertically' to God, who calls for our total reverence and love. The two widows are nothing less than role models in the matter of loving our neighbour and loving our God. May we draw inspiration from these two, anonymous women: the widow in Sidon who cared for Elijah and the widow in Jerusalem whom Jesus singled out for special praise.

The passion story from Mark's Gospel is a gripping read. What makes it just that are two pervasive patterns. First, a series of people take action against Jesus and 'hand him over'. Second, Jesus himself, right through Mark's passion story, remains utterly alone.

First, even before the Last Supper, Judas has decided to 'betray' or 'hand Jesus over' to the chief priests (Mark

14:10, 11, 21, 42, 44). Then the Sanhedrin, led by the high priest Caiaphas and the other priests, act against Jesus by having him bound and handed over to Pilate (Mark 15:1, 10). Finally, the Roman prefect Pontius Pilate acts against Jesus by having him 'scourged' and by 'handing him over to be crucified' (Mark 15:15).

It is not difficult to identify motives that prompted the actions of Caiaphas and Pilate. Unprincipled and cruel, Pilate took the easy way out in the cause of maintaining public order. Caiaphas and the chief priests were sure that they knew the truth. They found it blasphemous that Jesus had implicitly claimed to be on a par with God by forgiving sins, changing the divine law, and the rest. In any case he had disturbed the way they had combined business and worship in the running of the Temple. The motivation of Judas for betraying Jesus is harder to pin down. But we can say this: Pilate, Caiaphas, and Judas stood in for the whole human race in bringing about the death of Jesus. We can spot in them the moral weaknesses that prompt us into doing evil or failing to do the good we should. Like them and for our own 'good reasons', we too can 'hand Jesus over'.

Second, when Jesus was arrested, all his disciples 'deserted him and fled'. For a few minutes a mysterious 'young man' followed him. When the armed police tried to seize him as well, he left his garment in their hands and fled naked into the night (Mark 14:50–52). Whatever guesses we might make about his identity, the young man who ran away naked into the darkness powerfully symbolises the failure of Jesus' male disciples.

Peter had spoken for these disciples when he said to Jesus, 'we have left everything and followed you' (Mark 10:28; see Chapter 14 above). Now an anonymous young man, presumably also a disciple of Jesus, left his clothing behind as fear drove him away from Jesus. He 'left all things' to escape from the presence of Jesus.

From that moment in Mark's passion story, Jesus remains utterly isolated and undefended. No one speaks up for him and pleads his cause, let alone does anything for him. From the time of leaving the Passover supper until the moment of his death on the cross, Jesus receives no visible human support from anyone. He never sees a friendly face. There is a chilling loneliness to the unfolding story: his arrest, the proceedings he faces before Caiaphas and Pilate, and the death he endures when he cries out, 'My God, my God, why have you forsaken me?'

One horrific episode in Mark's passion story symbolises the way Jesus is delivered up to his enemies: his being flogged, crowned with thorns, and then mocked by a squad of soldiers. Like Matthew and John, Mark reports the scourging in a single word. He does not need to comment. His first-century readers know only too well what that punishment does to a person. Some of them will have seen what criminals and rebels look like after they have been scourged. Two soldiers systematically use spiked whips to flay the skin off the back of condemned men.

As Mark tells the passion story, it is not until after Jesus' death that anyone takes a stand for him. Seeing the way he died, the officer in charge of the execution squad declares, 'Truly this man was God's Son!' Only at this point in the narrative does Mark refer to a number of female followers of Jesus who have witnessed his crucifixion. He names three of them: Mary Magdalene, Mary the mother of James the younger and of Joses, and Salome (Mark 15:39–41). Thanks to them, the loneliness of Jesus in his suffering and death has not been complete.

The whole story of Jesus' arrest, suffering, death, and burial unfolds with breathless speed. From Mark's passion narrative, I have selected two themes and aimed at clarifying their nuances and deeper meaning. That can help us to take things in slow motion, let ourselves share vividly in what happened, and reflect deliberately: 'Yes, I was there when they crucified my Lord.'

LUKE'S GOSPEL

EIGHTEEN

Mary, Zachariah, Simeon and Anna

Recently I attended an international conference on inter-faith dialogue. The speakers came from all over the world and had many good things to say. One speaker, for instance, talked about the way our personal identity is shaped by others and, especially, by their love. We could apply that insight to the story of the visitation (Luke 1:39–56).

The identity of Mary is shaped or at least revealed and strengthened by another, Elizabeth her older cousin. Elizabeth asks: 'Why has this happened to me, that the mother of my Lord has come to me?' (Luke 1:43). Elizabeth calls her young cousin 'the mother of my Lord'. And that's what Mary is: the mother of the divine Lord of Elizabeth, who is also the Lord of all of us.

The Lord is with Mary, and is growing in her womb. It is the Lord who has shaped forever the unique identity of Mary. By her question, Elizabeth reveals and, in a way, shapes the identity of Mary for all time. It is as 'the mother of my Lord' and the mother of our Lord that we honour Mary in the feast of the Visitation.

On 22 December and 24 December, respectively, the Gospel is the *Magnificat* (Luke 1:46–55) and the *Benedictus* (Luke 1:68–79). We hear and use those wonderful hymns on many other occasions during the year.

Mary's hymn, the *Magnificat*, and Zachariah's hymn, the *Benedictus*, are both great songs of praise, praise that we express to God our Saviour. They differ in several ways. The *Magnificat* is, for example, more personal. It uses 'my' and 'me' five times, and slips into the plural only once: God 'spoke to our ancestors'. The *Benedictus* uses 'us' and 'our' ten times, and never 'me' and 'my'. The *Benedictus* focuses more on the people, while the *Magnificat* focuses more on Mary herself.

Yes, the perspectives of the *Magnificat* and the *Benedictus* differ somewhat. But they both converge in praising God. Whether we pray and think more individually or pray and think more collectively, Christmas means pouring out praise and thanks to God our Saviour who has come 'to visit us from on high'. But this is only a prelude. Such praise and thanks should also fill our minds and hearts right through the whole year.

When Mary and Joseph bring the Christ Child to present him in the Temple (Luke 2:22–40), they meet two old people, Simeon and Anna. When we celebrate on 2 February the Presentation, the feast highlights naturally the Christ Child. But it highlights also an old man and a very old woman.

The Holy Spirit 'rested on' Simeon, and 'it had been revealed to him by the Holy Spirit that he would not see death before he had seen the Lord's Messiah' (Luke 2:25, 26). Because the Spirit guided him, Simeon came into the Temple, took the Christ Child in his arms and spoke prophetically. Anna also came up and started speaking like the prophetess that she was (Luke 2:36). She 'began to praise God and speak about the child to all who were looking for the redemption of Jerusalem'.

Interestingly, in the story of the Presentation we are not told that the Holy Spirit revealed things to Mary and Joseph and gave them any special prompting. We do not hear, for instance, that they began to speak prophetically. What we do learn is that, when they carried the Christ Child to Jerusalem, they were following 'the law of the Lord'. In fact, this passage of Luke's Gospel tells us five times that Mary and Joseph acted according to the law of Moses or the law of the Lord (Luke 2:22, 23, 24, 27, 39).

It is also noteworthy that Mary and Joseph have nothing to say when they bring the Child into the Temple. They remain silent. It is the old people, Simeon and Anna, who are inspired by the Holy Spirit and have something prophetic to say.

Old people today may also be guided in a special way by the Holy Spirit, and may have something prophetic to tell us. Let us attend to the older folk. It just could be that they have important messages for all of us – even something very special to say to us about Jesus himself, as did Simeon and Anna.

NINETEEN

Pointing to Jesus, Losing Jesus and Loving Enemies

It is written . . . , 'The voice of one crying out in the wilderness: "Prepare the way of the Lord. Make his paths straight . . . and all flesh shall see the salvation of God"' (Luke 3:4, 6).

Many of my readers will have seen the painting of the crucifixion by Matthias Grünewald. It was attached to an altar in Isenheim but is now in a museum at Colmar (France). One side of the work shows a scene of sharp pain and disturbance. Mary Magdalene is tormented with grief; the Blessed Virgin Mary is collapsing into the arms of the beloved disciple. On the other side, the calm figure of John the Baptist gestures at Christ on the cross.

Of course, at the time of the crucifixion John the Baptist was well and truly dead. Months or even several years before, he had been beheaded in the dungeon of Herod Antipas. But Grünewald's painting sums up the life and ministry of John. He constantly pointed away from himself and pointed to Jesus.

Far from being centred on himself, John did not refer to himself. To use an adjective to which Pope Francis has given currency, John was not 'self-referential'. His existence was centred on Jesus and he was engaged in preparing for his coming.

Let us pray that our own lives may be totally centred on Jesus. Let us point away from ourselves, and point people to Jesus. From being self-referential, Lord Jesus, deliver us. Lord Jesus, let us become point-persons for you.

The Bible contains many wonderful passages that can fill us with joy. But there are also tragic stories that can leave us feeling sad, even very sad. For me, some of the saddest, even most tragic, words come at the end of Luke's account of Jesus being rejected in Nazareth (Luke 4:16-30). A murderous crowd hustle Jesus to the edge of a cliff on which the town is built; they want to throw him down to his death. But he 'slips through' the middle of the lynching party and 'walks away'.

At the end, the people are simply left without Jesus. He has grown up with them, lived among them, and has been preaching in their synagogue. But now he simply walks away from them all. He is gone and no longer there with them. They have lost his presence. What a tragic gap he leaves! What a terrible loss they have suffered!

The final sentence in that story reminds me of what Thomas à Kempis wrote in *The Imitation of Christ*: 'To be with Jesus is a delightful paradise. To be without Jesus is the pain of hell.'

When I read that sentence in Luke 4:30, all I can do is pray: 'Lord Jesus, may you never go away. Don't let us lose you. Without you, life is empty and tragic. Stay with us, despite all our sins and failures. Please, never leave us behind.'

'Love your enemies, do good to those who hate you, bless those who curse you, pray for those who abuse you' (Luke 6:27, 28).

Here we come to some of the impossible demands Jesus made of his disciples. Love your enemies; don't merely tolerate them. Do good to those who hate you; don't merely avoid hating them in return. Bless those who curse you; don't merely keep your mouth shut and refrain from cursing them in return. Pray for those who treat you badly; give them a special place in your prayers.

Jesus asks for something quite extraordinary. He asks his followers to behave in an astonishing way, which normal human reason and virtue could never suggest or support.

He wants us to aim at being like God himself: 'Be merciful, just as your Father is merciful' (Luke 6:36). That's a startling demand to make of us. Let us pray that Jesus may give us the strength and courage to share and imitate the very compassion of God.

TWENTY

On Not Judging, Raising the Dead and Showing Love

'Do not judge and you will not be judged' (Luke 6:37). This is another one of Jesus' heroic demands.

He doesn't add any qualifications. He doesn't, for instance, say: 'Unless there are obvious reasons, do not judge.' Or: 'Do not judge unless you have first-hand evidence to back up your judgements.' No, he simply states without qualification, 'Do not judge'.

This is a further 'hard saying' coming from Jesus, like 'love your enemies'. Common sense doesn't help us here. What reasons do we have for loving our enemies? Why should we refrain from judging other people?

The only force that will accept and practise such heroic demands will be our personal relationship with Jesus. Nothing less than a deep relationship with him can make it possible to love our enemies, to stop judging other people, and to practise further radical invitations Jesus puts to us. May the good Jesus strengthen our relationship with him. May he give us the courage to live the kind of life he expects from us.

The highpoint of the story of Jesus bringing back to life a young man (Luke 7:11–17) comes when we read that Jesus' 'heart went out to' the widowed mother. Often this verb is translated a little weakly: Jesus 'felt sorry' or 'had compassion' on her. But the original Greek is stronger and more vivid than that: Jesus' heart went out to her; he had a gut feeling of love for her.

Now Jesus had never met this woman before, nor did he know her dead son. The story is much shorter than the raising of the dead Lazarus in Bethany (John 11:1–44). Lazarus was a dear friend of Jesus, as were the two sisters Lazarus had left behind at his death. The story of Lazarus deals at length with the personal relations between Jesus and the family in Bethany. In Nain, however, Jesus did not know either the widow or her dead son.

The widow herself took no initiative in asking Jesus to do something for her, still less for her dead son. In her terrible grief, she never went looking for Jesus. In fact, she may never have even heard of him.

Seemingly by chance, Jesus ran into the widow on her way to the cemetery. His heart went out to her. His powerful love brought the young man to life, and Jesus gave him back to his mother.

In the twentieth century, an outstanding French philosopher, Gabriel Marcel, often wrote about such central themes of human existence as love. According to Marcel, to say to someone 'I love you' is tantamount to saying 'you will not die'. Yes, we do say to our dearest relatives and friends 'I love you'. But sadly they die. Our love for them remains, but it seems powerless in the face of death. Our parents, spouses, and other people very close to us pass away. All we can do is put them in a coffin, pray for them, and bury or cremate them. Face to face with death, our love is powerless.

But with Jesus it was and is different. The widow had lost her husband, and now had lost her only son. The heart of Jesus went out to her spontaneously. His word of love transformed the whole situation: 'Young man, I say to you, rise!' The love of Jesus is uniquely powerful. It proves stronger even than the final forces of death.

With a gut feeling of love, the heart of Jesus goes out to each one of us. To everyone he says 'I love you'. He shows a passionate love for each one of us. That love means that we too can share in his victory over death.

For some centuries people used to wear a Latin saying on brooches and other pieces of jewellery: '*amor vincit omnia*' ('love conquers all things'). This saying applies wonderfully well to Jesus himself; his love does conquer all things. For the widow of Nain and for all of us, his love comes into play to overcome everything, including death itself. We can always be sure that the heart of Jesus will never cease going out to each of us.

In modern times, the false idea has spread that love is only a feeling, an individual's passionate feeling or, as academics might say, 'subjective disposition'. Fortunately some philosophers and theologians have maintained and developed the notion of love as a relationship, a mutual relationship between persons. For such thinkers, love remains essentially a two-way street, giving and receiving, a relating in two directions.

Love is the key theme in the story told by Luke 7:36–50. It is a genuine, mutual love that shows itself in giving and receiving. That kind of love enfolds the whole story.

First, a woman who is a notorious sinner enters the dining room at the home of Simon the Pharisee and behaves towards Jesus with extravagant love. She washes his feet with her tears, dries his feet with her hair, and anoints his feet with precious ointment from an alabaster jar.

To deal with the scandalised reaction of his host, Jesus tells the story of a creditor who has two debtors: one owes him 500 denarii and the other only 50. (A denarius was the normal day's wage for a labourer.) When they could not pay, the creditor generously, even lovingly, cancels both debts. The two debtors love him in return, but the debtor who has owed 500 denarii loves the generous creditor even more. Then Jesus turns to praise the sinful woman: 'she has shown great love'.

Here Jesus says something about her that he never says about anyone else in the four Gospels: 'she has shown much love'. Some people invite Jesus to meals, like Simon the Pharisee. Others speak well of Jesus, notably

Simon Peter when he identifies Jesus as 'the Christ, the Son of the living God'. Others are closely bound to Jesus, like Martha, Mary, and their brother Lazarus – not to mention Jesus' own mother and the mysterious beloved disciple in John's Gospel. But what the sinful woman in Luke 7 does for Jesus prompts him into saying what he never says about anyone else: 'she has shown much love'.

This chapter of Luke presents us with an exceptional story of mutual love: the woman's extravagant love for Jesus and his generous, forgiving love towards her. He displays his love by what he says of her and by forgiving her sins. But he also receives love from her, and is glad to accept her love.

In his 2006 encyclical letter, 'God is Love', Pope Benedict XVI highlighted the way love involves receiving as well as giving. Love includes both need and benevolence – the need to receive love and benevolence in exercising love. Love entails not only giving to others and doing things for them but also receiving love from them.

Jesus' generous love makes him do wonderful things for the sinful woman. He defends her against self-righteous critics appalled that Jesus has allowed her to wash and anoint his feet. He speaks *for her* and praises her ('she has shown much love'). He speaks *to her* by forgiving her sins and praising her once again, this time for her faith: 'Your faith has saved you; go in peace.' Jesus' love for her makes him ready to act and speak on her behalf, just as it makes him ready to forgive us, defend us, and even die for us.

But Jesus also receives love from this anonymous, sinful woman. He wants her love; he needs her love. He also wants our love; he needs our love. He longs to be loved by us, greatly loved and even extravagantly loved by us.

We might join the woman in our prayer, kneeling at the feet of Jesus, even imagining that we weep some tears of joy and gratitude, even imagining that we too wipe his feet with our hair and join her in anointing his feet with some precious ointment that we have brought. Of course, it could seem unusual for us to exercise our imagination that way in prayer. But Jesus wants our love. He would be only too happy if we were to kneel at his feet with that woman who showed him such great love.

TWENTY-ONE

Transfiguration, Foxes and Birds, and the Sending of the 72

When Luke tells the story of the transfiguration (Luke 9:28–36), he specifies that Jesus 'went up on the mountain to pray'. It was 'while he was praying' that his face changed, his clothing shone brilliantly, and Moses and Elijah appeared 'in glory' to speak with him about his 'departure' or coming death, resurrection, and ascension.

Peter, James, and John had climbed the mountain with Jesus for some quiet prayer, and now found themselves sharing an intense religious experience. Right there in front of them, Jesus was transfigured, and the three disciples 'saw his glory'. Two people who went the distance for God joined him: Moses, representing the law, and Elijah, the prophets. During their lifetime, Moses and Elijah had seen the glory of God; now they appear with Jesus in glory.

The Bible has much to say about the 'glory' or radiant splendour of God, as something that is very close to the divine beauty. When the psalmist declares, 'The heavens are telling the glory of God' (Psalm 19:1), this amounts to saying, 'The heavens are telling the beauty of God.' After the destruction of the city, Isaiah promises that, when Jerusalem is restored, the luminous beauty of God will appear over it (Isaiah 60:1–5). Not only in the heavens above but also in the holy city here on earth, the beauty of God can be seen.

At the transfiguration Peter, James, and John saw in advance something of the glorious beauty that would shine forth from Christ when raised from the dead. Their hearts were on fire. Hardly knowing what he was saying, Peter volunteered to prolong and preserve this enthralling vision of beauty by making three dwellings: one for Jesus, one for Moses, and one for Elijah.

Peter reacted in a way we all do when carried away by some enchanting experience. Years ago at the Salzburg Festival, the young Claudio Abbado set on fire the hearts of a huge audience by brilliantly conducting Beethoven's Seventh Symphony. Along with thousands of others who had come from around the world, I did not want that experience of beauty to end. We can all remember such intense experiences that made us incredibly happy, experiences that we wanted to last forever.

But more was to come for Peter, James, and John. A cloud swept over them and terrified them. From the shining cloud came the voice of God: 'This is my Son, my Chosen; listen to him!' The three disciples were uniquely privileged. They saw the future beauty of Christ unveiled before their eyes; they heard the very voice of God.

Before the three disciples had time to digest inwardly their awesome experience, it suddenly ended. Moses and Elijah disappeared; the cloud was gone; the divine voice fell silent; the radiant beauty slipped away from the face and body of Jesus. Quite abruptly the three disciples found themselves alone with their Master on the mountain.

When they came down from the mountain, they took to heart the vision of Christ's divine beauty they had been granted. From now on, they could focus their attention on the glorious Son of God and give him their lifelong devotion.

On our own journey through life, every now and then we may feel like the character in *Humboldt's Gift*, a novel by Saul Bellow. Life for him is a nightmare during which he is trying to get some sleep. Or, to quote a question from the Roman philosopher Seneca: 'Why weep for the end of life? The whole of it deserves our tears.'

Jesus deals with our nightmares and our tears. We enjoy the sure knowledge of his triumph over death on the cross, the 'departure' which Moses and Elijah spoke of at the transfiguration. This departure became Jesus' passage to a glory that will never end.

The last book of the Bible, the Book of Revelation, fills out the glimpse of glory conveyed by Jesus' transfiguration. God will make a home among human beings, and will 'wipe every tear from their eyes. Death will be no more; mourning and crying and pain will be no more.' These things will have passed away. A cosmic transformation will bring 'a new heaven and a new earth' (Revelation 21:1–4).

The transfiguration of Jesus led on to his glorious, heavenly transformation. What he experienced on the mountain promised that such a transformation would be his destiny and the destiny of those who follow him. The God who spoke to the three disciples on the mount of transfiguration is utterly faithful to those who find in him 'their light and their salvation'.

Let us constantly go up the mountain to pray with Jesus. May we too see something of his divine beauty that will set our hearts on fire. When we do, we will be able to focus our attention on him and give him our lifelong allegiance.

A man on the road said to Jesus, '"I will follow you wherever you go." Jesus answered: "Foxes have holes, and birds of the air have nests; but the Son of Man has nowhere to lay his head"' (Luke 9:57, 58).

These are the painful words with which Jesus, the Son of Man, drew a contrast between himself and foxes and birds, and pictured how he lived his life in constant danger. Foxes dig holes in the ground. They are safe when they stay hidden away deep down in their burrows. Birds of the air perch in their nests high up in trees. They can be more or less free of danger up there, out of range of cats and other marauders.

But Jesus had no nest up a tree and out of danger. He had no hole in the ground, no secure bunker where he could be safe. Sometimes he slept rough, lying on the ground under the stars. Jesus was not as safe as birds of the air or foxes in their holes. He didn't have a fixed home, not even one like the birds and foxes. As someone described his situation, he spent the last years of his earthly life out there on open ground, under fire. Jesus lived a homeless and very vulnerable life, a life that lacked normal defences and was constantly exposed to danger and attack.

At the end they came to get him. He died stretched out on a cross, without a roof over his head and far from any home he could call his own. What he said about lacking even the protection birds and foxes enjoy proved terribly true when his life shut down. He lived that life and died that death because he loved each one of us with all his heart, with a love stronger than death itself. It was love that exposed Jesus to danger and made him utterly vulnerable to his enemies.

Luke's Gospel doesn't explicitly use the word 'love'. But love is there crying out to be mentioned. The 'man on the road' says to Jesus, 'I will follow you wherever you go.' In effect, he is saying to Jesus, 'I love you and I will follow you wherever you go.' Jesus, in effect, says to him in reply, 'Yes, but how much do you love me? Are you ready to accept with me a dangerous, very vulnerable life that could end in violent death?'

Presumably everyone reading this book loves Jesus. You love him and want to follow him. Yet we must hear the question he asks us: 'How much do you love me? Do you love me more than you love anyone else in the world? Do you put me before anything else in the world, because you love me more than anything else in the world? Are you even ready to lose your life for my sake, because you love me more than life itself?'

In April 2016, Pope Francis flew down to the Greek island of Lesbos to visit many refugees who had escaped from situations of terrible danger. He heard the stories that some of them wanted to tell him. One man told the Pope about the death of his wife. She was a Christian and was not prepared to give up her faith in Jesus Christ. So she was beheaded in front of her children. In this awful way, she lost her life for the sake of Christ. She lost her life because she loved Christ more than life itself.

I write this chapter a few days after celebrating the birthday of the cousin of Jesus, John the Baptist, who grew up to be a martyr. Earlier in the same week we remembered two sixteenth-century martyrs, Thomas More and John Fisher. They put Jesus before anyone else or anything else in the world. They loved him and were willing to lose their lives for his sake. More and Fisher loved him more than life itself. Their strong love has not disappeared today. We see that love at work in the martyrs of our time. They put Jesus before anyone else in the world. They give their lives for Jesus because they love him and love all that he stands for.

A few days ago at the day care centre in Caritas Christi (Melbourne), I celebrated Mass in Italian for a group of old Italians who had come to Australia many years ago. A challenging response went with the psalm: 'Strong, O Lord, is your love for us (forte, Signore, è il tuo amore per noi).' We can join in that response and say, 'Strong, O Lord, is your love for us.' And we can pray to love him more and more. Let's ask that, like Thomas More, John Fisher, and that Christian woman in Syria, we might show in and through our lives that our love for him is truly a strong love, a love that puts Jesus before anything else in our world.

Luke offers us spiritual treasures, marvellous passages that are found only in his Gospel and have shaped Christian life, prayer, and imagination from the beginning. Down the ages, the parables of the Good Samaritan (Luke 10:29–37) and the rich man and Lazarus (Luke 16:19–31) have challenged believers to help the distressed and impoverished people they meet. Christian prayer has taken up the wonderful prayers with which Luke opens his story of Jesus: the *Magnificat* from the Virgin Mary (Luke 1:46–55), the *Benedictus* from Zachariah (Luke 1:68–79), and the *Nunc Dimittis* from Simeon (Luke 2:29–32). Artists have returned again and again to the scenes of the Annunciation (Luke 1:26–38) and the Nativity (Luke 2:1–20).

A further treasure comes with Luke's account of Jesus sending 72 disciples on a mission to announce the kingdom of heaven (Luke 10:1–12). What's so special about this story? It turns up in Luke's Gospel shortly after an episode that seems much more important: the commissioning and trial mission of the 12 (Luke 9:1–6). These 12 men formed a unique group who followed Jesus during his lifetime, became *the* official witnesses to his resurrection from the dead, and served as the founding fathers of the Church. They were already the leaders of the small Christian community when the Holy Spirit descended at the first Pentecost. Empowered by the Spirit, the 12 launched the spread of the Church.

The 12 apostles stand there as gigantic figures at the start of Christianity. It is not easy for us later Christians to identify with them. They seem larger than life, like the stained glass windows that portray them in some cathedrals or the huge statues of them that line the Basilica of St John Lateran in Rome.

Unlike the 12 apostles, the much larger group of 72 disciples sent out by Jesus during his ministry seem much closer to us. They went on mission in pairs, two by two. We do not learn their names. Were they all men? Probably not. A chapter earlier, Luke has mentioned such women as Mary Magdalene, Joanna, and Susanna (Luke 8:1–3). They were also disciples and travelled with Jesus during his ministry. The 72 sent on the mission could well have included some of the female disciples, maybe some married couples. We do not know this for sure, but we certainly cannot exclude the possibility.

What we do learn from Luke's Gospel is that Jesus gave a larger group of his followers, 72 of them, a missionary vocation. What happened to them later? Were some or even all of them among the 120 who gathered to pray in Jerusalem with Mary the mother of Jesus, Peter, and the other 12 apostles before the Holy Spirit came down on the whole community (Acts 1:12–15)? Presumably some of the 72 became leaders in the Christian Church after Pentecost. But we do not know any particulars.

What we do learn from Luke is that Jesus also gave a missionary task to a much wider group than the 12. We can easily identify imaginatively with that larger group, those rank and file disciples to whom he gave a triple task: to bring peace wherever they went, to heal the sick, and to preach the kingdom of God.

The commission given to the 72 disciples belongs to every baptised Christian. We are all to be people of peace, men and women who bring others the peace of Christ wherever we go. We too are called to serve others by caring for the sick, feeding the hungry, visiting the lonely, and encouraging the desperate. We too are called to proclaim the kingdom of God and tell people of the wonderful new life that Jesus has brought into the world.

The story of the sending of the 72 vividly reminds us of what we should all do as missionaries for Christ. We can turn this story into a prayer of self-examination. Do I bring the peace of Christ wherever I go? Do I care for the sick and the needy? Do I spread the word about the blessings that come through the person and presence of Jesus Christ?

TWENTY-TWO

Prophets and Kings, a Tax Collector, and Love

' . . . many prophets and kings desired to see what you see, but did not see it, and to hear what you hear, but did not hear it' (Luke 10:24).

Jesus is speaking here of the incredible blessing the disciples received when, over and over again for several years, they saw what he did in working miracles and heard what he said in preaching the kingdom of God along the roads of Galilee. A similar blessing belongs also to the followers of Jesus today.

Think of what we see and hear right under our noses. Think of what we see and hear in our daily existence – through so many things in the lives of all those around us who love and serve Jesus. Love shown in family life constantly reflects the love he inspires and empowers. Other men and women, young and old, bring us into his presence and let us hear his voice.

Think of what we see and hear when we join others for worship. We see people kneel in devout prayer or walk up to receive Christ in Holy Communion. We see the vivid face of a small child who has just received Communion for the first time. We catch the happiness that shines forth from a couple who pledge themselves to each other in the presence of the Lord.

We can also see the face of Jesus when we look into the faces of the homeless, the dying, asylum seekers, victims of domestic violence, unloved children and those in jail. As Blaise Pascal expressed this ongoing passion of the Lord, 'He is in agony until the end of the world, and we must not sleep during all that time.'

We hear the Scriptures read, hymns sung, and preachers speaking to us of our loving Lord. The words of a hymn, a psalm, or some passage from the Gospels may bring us the voice of Jesus.

Every now and then films have a similar impact. Here I am thinking not so much of such straightforward Jesus-films as Franco Zeffirelli's *Jesus of Nazareth* or Mel Gibson's *The Passion of the Christ*. Indirectly the voice and face of Christ may come through other films, like the French film *Of Gods and Men*, the Irish film *Calvary*, and the Italian film *God Willing*.

What we see and hear can bring us into the presence of Jesus and let us hear his voice or even see his face. This should fill us with gratitude and prompt us into thanking our God for blessing us through all that we see and hear of Jesus as our life unfolds.

My thoughts on the parable of the self-righteous Pharisee and the sinful tax collector (Luke 18:9–14) were permanently changed in 1989 by a massacre that happened on 16 November in El Salvador. Father Ignacio Ellacuria, five other Jesuits, their cook, and her little daughter were dragged out of their beds and were shot to death on the lawn of their residence by the security forces. Around the world, plaques in the form of a cross list the eight names.

A few weeks before they were killed, at a community meeting the six Jesuits reflected together on this parable. They questioned themselves: 'Are we really better than the Pharisee? We think we know the real problems that are tearing this country apart. Inspired by liberation theology, we are working to solve these problems. But are we doing this in the spirit of "we know better than our critics"? Deep down are we radically self-righteous?' In a thoughtful and detailed way, the six priests asked the question: 'Do we pride ourselves on being better in our theory and practice than those who criticise and oppose us?'

A visiting Jesuit attended that community meeting and then went on to Rome for further studies. A few days after the six Jesuits and the two women were murdered, he told me the story of that community meeting in El Salvador.

The way in which Ellacuria and his companions questioned themselves marked their real greatness and holiness. If these courageous friends of Jesus saw the danger of lining up with the Pharisee in Jesus' story, so should others who read that parable.

Those martyred Jesuits felt the temptation of lapsing into thinking: 'We are not like other people. Look at the good, even heroic things we are saying and writing in the cause of peace and justice.' Each of them wanted to deal meticulously with this temptation, join the tax collector, and say with utter sincerity 'God, be merciful to me, a sinner.'

What is God like? The most beautiful story Jesus ever told set itself to answer that question (Luke 15:11–32). It would be better to call this the Parable of the Merciful Father rather than the Parable of the Prodigal Son (or even the Parable of the Lost Son). To be sure, other parables also throw light on what God is like. But this parable radically challenges our understanding of God in ways that form a defining moment in recognising what God is like.

The First Letter of John never mentions this parable but sums up very precisely what it is about: 'God is love' (1 John 4:8, 16). Love is the most fundamental characteristic of God. What this letter states succinctly comes deployed at length in the Parable of the Merciful Father.

Some or even many readers will have seen *The Theory of Everything*, a 2014 film of the life of Stephen Hawking. Like other theoretical physicists and cosmologists, he has searched for the 'grand unified theory' of everything (GUT). Jesus would encourage us to find our grand unified theory in the divine love itself.

God's love is the bond that reconciles, forgives, and holds all people and things together. One might even boldly say that God is our GUT. God wants to do nothing less than hold all of us together in the divine love.

In the Parable of the Merciful Father, Jesus tells an astonishing, unsettling story, a story of the love that characterises God. The parable invites us to recognise and to accept the divine love that is always welcoming, life-giving and the source of lasting joy.

TWENTY-THREE

Hanging on Words, Being Alive and Ascending to Heaven

'The people hung on his words' (Luke 19:48 NIV). Every now and then we see people doing just that – hanging on the words of someone.

One of the loveliest things in family life is what happens when a mother or a father reads some gripping story to their little children. I remember one young mother reading a book to her two daughters and twin sons. They clustered around her, listened ever so intently, and hung upon every word that came from Sylvia's mouth. I think of a young father telling stories to his two daughters when they had gone to bed. Susan and Naomi hung upon Jim's words until their heads began to nod and they fell asleep.

Adults do the same. When her children come home from school, I notice Victoria hanging upon their words when they tell her what has happened to them that day. Or we can think of young men who have fallen in love. You see them hanging upon every word their beloved says to them.

That's what Jesus' audience in Jerusalem did when he preached to them. They hung upon every word he uttered. He became the total centre of their attention. They found him enthralling; they couldn't take their eyes off him; they hung upon everything he said.

May Jesus take possession of our lives, so that we let him become the enthralling centre of our attention. Let us hang upon every word he says to us. He is utterly precious, and every word that comes from him must be treasured as utterly precious.

Luke left us a masterpiece in the Easter story that he told of two disciples walking with the risen Jesus for hours and then coming to recognise him at Emmaus in the breaking of the bread (Luke 24:13–35). The account of this meeting with Jesus is superbly constructed. The real highpoint of the story comes halfway through. The disciples, who have not yet recognised him, tell Jesus that the women had been told by the angels: 'he is alive'. It is a supreme irony. Without knowing who he is, they tell Jesus that he is alive. And there he is alive and walking with them!

That's the heart of the matter. Jesus is gloriously alive, and wants to share his wonderful, new life with each one of us.

Luke likes using the word 'life' in this part of his narrative about Jesus. When women visit the tomb where Jesus was buried, two angels speak with one voice and ask

'Why do you seek the living among the dead?' Luke does not drop the language of Jesus being raised or rising from the dead. But he emphasises what the resurrection has led to: 'he is alive'.

Luke wants to remind his readers of what followed the event of the resurrection. Jesus is gloriously alive. Risen from the dead, he now enjoys wonderful, new life. He is alive *in himself*, but also very much alive *for us*. He wants to share with us his transformed, glorious existence. He is the Life-giver. The Creed calls the Holy Spirit 'Lord and Life-giver'. But Jesus himself is also just that: our risen Lord and our Life-giver.

The story of Jesus and the two disciples on the road to Emmaus reaches its core statement when the disciples report the words of the angels: 'he is alive'. Jesus is gloriously alive and wants to draw us into his new existence. We can only pray: 'Jesus, it is marvellous that you are alive and live forever. Give each of us an ever richer share in your risen existence.'

Many years ago, a doctoral student in Rome presented and defended his dissertation, which concerned the account of Jesus' ascension found in the final verses of Luke's Gospel (Luke 24:50–53). I was fortunate to be there, in the role of president for the board of examiners.

I say 'fortunate', because in the course of the discussion a richly illuminating insight emerged. As many readers notice, Luke offers much for Christian prayer. Right from the opening chapters, where we have the *Magnificat*, the *Benedictus*, and the *Nunc Dimittis*, this Gospel introduces the theme of prayer. But down to the end, you never hear of the disciples of Jesus actually praying. They learn about prayer. Jesus teaches them a brief form of the Lord's Prayer (Luke 11:1–4). But we never find them engaged in prayer.

Then, right at the very end, Jesus blesses them and is carried up into heaven. They go back to Jerusalem, full of joy, and are continually in the Temple praising God. They have been blessed by Jesus risen from the dead. This fills them with joy. For the first time in Luke's Gospel, they give themselves to praying and praising God.

Easter joy and the blessing of the risen Jesus release something within the disciples, triggering constant prayer. They have crossed a boundary to begin a life of prayer.

May that be the experience of all of us. May the blessing of the living Christ and Easter joy set us free to pray constantly and join in praising always our loving God.

JOHN'S GOSPEL

TWENTY-FOUR

Born Again, Loving the World and Replacing the Passover

What does Nicodemus expect from Jesus when he comes to meet him under cover of darkness (John 3:1–15)? Nicodemus has already reached some conclusions about Jesus: 'Rabbi, we know that you are a teacher come from God, for no one can do these signs that you do unless God is with him' (John 3:2 ESV). Apparently, Nicodemus simply wants some reassurance and confirmation that Jesus truly is a divinely endorsed teacher.

But what happens in the conversation with Jesus suddenly goes beyond the limited agenda Nicodemus has set. Jesus abruptly informs him: 'unless one is born again he cannot see the kingdom of God'. Jesus presses on and spells out this unexpected invitation. To enter the kingdom of God, one needs new birth through water and the Holy Spirit.

Nicodemus knows or at least thinks he knows what can happen and what cannot happen. The words 'how' and 'can' recur in three questions he asks, and suggest a limited view of God's power. '*How can* anyone be born after having grown old? *Can* one enter a second time into his mother's womb and be born? *How can* these things be?' (John 3:4, 9 emphasis added).

Nicodemus is a sincerely religious man, but also, seemingly, a rigid person who has life under control. For the time being he has only a limited trust in the power of the Holy Spirit. But he will eventually change, defending Jesus before those in authority (John 7:50–52) and at the end joining Joseph of Arimathea to ensure that Jesus receives a royal burial (John 19:38–42).

Like Nicodemus, we cannot remain closed against questioning and with only a limited view of God's power. We don't need to be rigid and keep life under our control. Like Nicodemus, we must learn how in our own lives the invisible Spirit of God blows where he wills.

I am grateful that in what he says to Nicodemus, Jesus links 'water' with the Holy Spirit. Last year the arrival of a large, green tank in the grounds of the college where I live turned water into a more vivid symbol for me. Winter rain from our roofs filled the tank. During the hot days of the summer, sufficient water was available to refresh our back garden and bring it new life. The lawns and shrubs could flourish, and not die under the blazing summer sun of Australia.

Water and the Holy Spirit come into play at our baptismal initiation, when we are born into the life of the triune God. That is a hugely significant event, and yet it is only the point of departure from our old life into our new life with God. We need to be constantly nourished 'from above' and enlivened by the Spirit. The green tank at my back door remains an ever-present reminder of the Holy Spirit's work in providing new, refreshing life day by day.

In one of the most famous statements in the Scriptures, John's Gospel says, 'God so loved the world that he gave his only Son, so that everyone who believes in him may not perish but may have eternal life' (John 3:16). I can still hear the voice of Billy Graham quoting those words when he came to the highpoint of a powerful sermon. Around the same time, someone sent me a card that commented on the verse by saying, 'God cared enough to send the best'.

We might also comment on that verse in another way and say: 'As far as God is concerned, nothing but the very best is good enough for each of us.'

Yes, God truly cared enough to send the best. As far as God is concerned, nothing but the very best is good enough for us.

The only miracle worked by Jesus that all four Gospels report is the feeding of the 5000 (John 6:1–15). Many readers will know that already. But they may not have noticed one or two significant differences in the way John tells the story.

Significantly, John begins by recalling that this crowd had come to see and hear Jesus shortly before the central Jewish festival, the Passover, took place. Instead of heading for Jerusalem to celebrate the Passover, they headed for Galilee to be with Jesus and immerse themselves completely in his presence. For them, he had taken the place of the central, religious feast that Jews treasured so deeply.

For us, may Jesus take the place of our feasts and all those things we treasure intensely. Like the 5000 on the shores of the Sea of Galilee, may we too experience what Jesus will do for us if we let him take the place of everything we prize greatly. Jesus will feed us and satisfy us in a way that no one else can.

Let us head for Jesus and say, 'May we find in you something so precious that no one else and nothing else will really count. You are the most precious treasure in our lives. You give a depth and meaning to our existence that we find nowhere else.'

TWENTY-FIVE

On Giving Thanks, Not Being Afraid and Finding Life

'Jesus took the loaves, and when he had given thanks (*eucharistēsas*), he distributed them to those who were seated' (John 6:11).

Recently I was talking with a holy, old woman from India, who turned out to be the sister of Anthony de Mello, an acclaimed spiritual writer and teacher who died too young in 1987. She insisted that we should always be very grateful for all the good things God constantly gives us and does for us. 'What do you mean by that?' I asked her. 'Well,' Grace replied, 'when we get up in the morning, we should thank God that we have eyes with which to see. We have ears with which to hear. We have feet with which we can walk.'

She paused and went on: 'When we get up in the morning, we've been asleep. Our bodies are now refreshed, and we are still functioning properly. God has given us another day, another beautiful day. Let's thank God for that and for many other things as well.'

I was glad to hear what my friend from India had to say over lunch. She made me think of another meal, the Eucharist, the special act of thanksgiving we make together to God. That's what 'Eucharist' means – giving thanks, and, more specifically, giving thanks to God through Christ and in the Spirit for all the great and beautiful gifts we have received. God has given us his Son as our Brother and Saviour, and so much else besides, beginning with the gift of the Holy Spirit.

Every day and, above all, at the Eucharist, we should pour out our thanks for the blessings that come our way and show us how much God loves us.

As readers can see above, John chose *'eucharistēsas'* rather than the word we find when the other Gospels describe the miraculous multiplication of the loaves: *'eulogēsen* (he blessed)'. All four evangelists draw some link between what Jesus did in feeding the 5000 and what he would do at his last meal on the night before he died. But by his choice of language, John makes a clearer link to the institution of the Eucharist.

The Eucharist has other names, like Communion, the (divine) Liturgy, the Lord's Supper, and the Mass. But the Eucharist has the advantage of suggesting the thanksgiving that includes all that Tony de Mello's sister mentioned and much else besides. If we look back, there are endless blessings to remember that we have received through our families, our communities and our Church. In the course of our lives, the good Lord has sent us so many blessings through the people who have cared for each of us. The Eucharist gives us the chance, repeatedly, to thank our loving God for giving us so much and, not least, Jesus, our crucified and risen Friend who lives with us always and remains constantly there at the heart of our lives.

Double meanings proliferate in John's Gospel. Things are said that contain not only an ordinary, 'surface' meaning but also a deeper, more astounding meaning. We find a typical example of this when the disciples struggled away with a strong wind out on the Sea of Galilee (John 6:16–21). Night had fallen and Jesus came towards their boat walking on the water. They were overwhelmed with fear at what they glimpsed in the darkness. But Jesus said to them: 'It is I; do not be afraid.'

At one level, it all makes good sense: 'It's me, the Jesus whom you know very well and with whom you have been travelling around Galilee.' But what Jesus says, *'egō eimi'*, could also be translated as 'I am'. That translation takes us back to Moses meeting God in the burning bush and God's self-presentation: 'I am' or 'I am who I am' (Exodus 3:1–15). When Jesus says, 'I am', he is also presenting himself in an awesome, divine way.

Those who look for clues and search for answers find here a remarkable example of a double meaning. Jesus says something that can be translated in two remarkably divergent ways. 'It's me; it's just me' or 'I am who I am. I am the One whom Moses encountered in the desert'.

This play of meanings, both surface and deeper, hints at the way God meets us and speaks to us both as the everyday God and the awesome God. God says: 'it's me, only me, the God in whom, day by day, you live and move and have your being' (see Acts 17:28). God also says: 'I am who I am. I am the mysterious God who comes to you in awesome moments, just as I revealed myself to Moses at the burning bush.'

Jesus himself is also just that: our everyday God and our awesomely mysterious God. He is the one (lower case) who says to us, 'It's me, only me.' He is also the One (upper case) who says to us, not in a blazing fire but in the darkness, 'I am. I am who I am.'

A story was told some years ago about a text inscribed on the tomb of a bishop (or was he a theologian?). The story was fictional but the message provocatively interesting. This is what it said.

'When I was young and free and my imagination had no limits, I dreamed of changing the world. As I grew older and wiser, I discovered the world would not change. So I shortened my sights somewhat and decided to change only my country. But it, too, seemed immovable. As I grew into my twilight years, in one last desperate attempt, I settled for changing those closest to me, my own family. But, alas, they would have none of it.

But now, as I lie on my deathbed, I suddenly and sadly realise that, if I had only changed myself first, then, by example, I would have changed my family. With their inspiration and encouragement, I would have been able to better my country. And, who knows, I may have even changed the world.'

The story contains a lot of truth. But one thing is untrue. We cannot change ourselves. Only our loving Lord Jesus can do that. Our job is to allow him to change us.

John's Gospel includes a long discourse on Jesus as 'the bread of life' (John 6:22-59). This bread nourishes us, changes us, and, through us, changes others. We must draw life from Jesus and let him feed us. Jesus, our food and our life, change us now and change us forever.

Jesus came to give us life, indeed the fullness of life (John 10:10). That is the theme of a prayer for each day that I picked up somewhere. Raking over my memories, I cannot recall its author. But here it is – in a slightly adjusted form.

'Jesus, you came to give us the fullness of life, for you said: "I have come so that they may have life and have it to the full." I want to take this invitation very seriously today. My life can never be repeated. What I will live today is gained forever. What I do not live today is lost forever.

Grant me a sense of my responsibility: to give all that I can give today, to love all whom I can love today, and to find thereby the deepest joy of living and giving, by following you on your path, which is the path of truth. In becoming myself, I will become everything in you.'

TWENTY-SIX

Mary, Judas, Peter, Love and Happiness

Many years ago in the Senate House at the University of Cambridge, I heard a philosopher turned novelist, Iris Murdoch, lecture on the supremacy of good. I admired her language, enjoyed the way she ran her fingers through her hair like one or two male conductors I had seen, and was intrigued by the way she linked the good and the beautiful.

She set me thinking about the way goodness shows itself to be beautiful and good, while evil often shows itself to be ugly, sordid and selfish. A dinner at Bethany hosted by Lazarus and his two sisters provides a vivid illustration of the difference (John 12:1–8).

Mary, one of Lazarus' two sisters, proves beautiful and generous in what she does for Jesus. She anoints his feet with costly ointment (probably imported from India) and then dries his feet with her hair. In all the history I have ever studied and all the literature I have ever read, I have only once come across another example of a woman drying someone's feet with her lovely hair. That was the case of the anonymous woman who also did that for Jesus (Luke 7:38; see Chapter 20 above).

Mary does something very beautiful and utterly generous. In John's account of the dinner, she is set over against Judas, described as a thief and someone who, despite his words ('Why was this ointment not sold for three hundred denarii and given to the poor?'), has no desire to help the needy. He cannot condone, let alone appreciate, the lovely gesture of Mary, who loves Jesus and is ever so grateful that he has brought her beloved brother Lazarus back to life.

Let us go down on our knees at the feet of Jesus, and pray to share more fully in Mary's lovely and generous love for him.

'The devil had already put it into the heart of Judas Iscariot . . . to betray [Jesus] . . . [Judas] immediately went out. And it was night' (John 13:2, 30).

Such passages in the story of Jesus' passion make sad reading. We hear how, after Satan entered the heart of Judas, he went out into the darkness of the night to betray Jesus. Judas had drifted apart from Jesus by becoming a thief, and that prepared the way for a final, terrible failure when he handed Jesus over to his ruthless enemies.

The failure of Judas is matched to some extent by that of Peter. He loved Jesus and was very close to him. But, despite being warned by Jesus (John 13:36–38), Peter became terrified at what might happen if he confessed to being a follower of Jesus. Three times he denied that he even knew Jesus (John 18:15–18, 25–27). Fear, rather than theft, led to Peter's failure.

It can be depressing to read what Judas and then Peter did; their stories more than hint at ways in which we all fail Jesus. That's the bad news. But the good news is much, much better. Jesus loves us all; he died and rose from the dead to save all of us. We fail and fall. But that never stops Jesus from loving us and picking us up again.

We can only look at him and pray: 'We adore you, O Christ, and we praise you, because by your holy cross you have redeemed the world, and you have redeemed me.'

A few months back I went with a grandniece to Her Majesty's Theatre for a performance of the musical *Strictly Ballroom*. An enthusiastic young audience made it all good fun, and we finished with the theme song 'Love is in the air'.

Many times in the Gospel of John, love is in the air. At the Last Supper, Jesus tells his disciples: 'I give you a new commandment, that you love one another' (John 13:34). Whether we read the last discourse of Jesus (John 13–17) or the whole of John's Gospel, we are persistently asked to dream big and find love.

Yet it all leaves us with the question: what is love? Where should we start in what we want to say about love? Undoubtedly there are very many things to say about love. But what's the first thing to say?

God helps us here, or at least the way God is portrayed in the opening chapter of the Bible. God creates the world and, finally, makes human beings, male and female.

And then the Bible says: 'God saw everything that he had made, and indeed, it was very good' (Genesis 1:31). When God looked at humankind he said it was very good. God loves each one of us, and says to each one of us, 'You are very good.'

That's the first thing we should emphasise about love. It means looking at other people and saying, 'You are very good. I am utterly glad that you exist. I am very happy that you are here.'

Beyond question, we have much more to say about love – about what love means and what love does. But love starts by looking at other human beings and thinking to ourselves or even saying to them, 'You are very good. I'm very glad you exist. I'm very glad you are here in my world.'

When we think and say just that, we can be quite certain that love is in the air – that Jesus' love is in the air.

Sometimes young people read a book, and its message stays with them for a lifetime. That's what happened to St Augustine of Hippo (d. 430). As a young student he read a book by the Roman lawyer and statesman Marcus Tullius Cicero (d. 43 BC) and he kept quoting it for many, many years. Centuries ago the book was lost. What we know of the text comes almost entirely from the quotations we find in the writings of Augustine. The book was called *Hortensius*, and it began from an absolutely certain starting-point: we all want to be happy.

In John's Gospel, after Jesus has washed and dried the feet of his disciples, he says to them: 'If you know these things, you are blessed if you do them' (John 13:17). The verse could also be translated: 'Now you know this [the example of Jesus in washing their feet], happiness will be yours if you behave accordingly.'

That's a startling promise: 'Happiness will be yours.' Yes, we all want to be happy. But what will bring us happiness? John's Gospel answers: happiness will be ours if we love and serve others, even (or especially?) in very humble ways, like Jesus washing the feet of his disciples.

The United States Declaration of Independence offers three examples of self-evident rights which God has given to human beings and which governments exist to protect: the rights to 'life, liberty, and the pursuit of happiness'. The third right implies that we can and should pursue happiness and directly aim at being happy, so long as we don't do anything illegal and violate the rights of others. For Jesus, however, happiness is not a pursuit of something we want for ourselves. It is rather what happens when we give ourselves to loving and serving others. Then happiness will be ours. We have his word for it.

TWENTY-SEVEN

Philip, Peace and Jesus the Vine

'Have I been with you all this time, Philip, and you still do not know me?' (John 14:9). To put this tough question in context, we need to retrace for a moment what we have already read in John's Gospel.

In the story of the feeding of the 5000, Jesus gave a special place to the apostle Philip. It was to him that Jesus turned and said: 'Where are we to buy bread for these people to eat?' The Gospel writer adds at once: '[Jesus] said this to test him, for he himself knew what he was going to do' (John 6:5, 6). Notice that Jesus did not clearly aim at testing all the disciples, but only Philip. He wanted Philip to take in what was about to happen when the people were miraculously fed. Jesus hoped that Philip, in particular, would learn something and grow spiritually.

Philip enjoyed a significant place in John's Gospel – right from the beginning. Back in Chapter 1 we learn that 'Jesus found Philip and said to him, "follow me"', and straightaway Philip recruited another disciple for Jesus, Nathanael (John 1:43–51). The calling of Philip set him apart from Andrew, Peter, and others. They went looking for Jesus but in the case of Philip, Jesus went looking for him. When he found Philip, Jesus recruited him by simply saying, 'follow me'.

Now at the Last Supper, Philip lets his desire to know God lead him to put a rather foolish request to Jesus: 'Lord, show us the Father and we will be satisfied.' This draws from Jesus a question which is both a response and a rebuke: 'Have I been with you all this time, Philip, and you still do not know me?' At once Jesus adds 'Whoever has seen me has seen the Father' (John 14:8, 9). Philip's request has in fact already been granted. But he has failed to grasp that through his person and work Jesus has been totally taken up with revealing the Father.

Philip has spent several years with Jesus. He has seen him working various miraculous signs – right from the revelation at Cana in Galilee (John 2:1–11). Philip has heard so much of Jesus' teaching. Philip played a cameo role in the feeding of the 5000. And yet he has not appreciated what Jesus has been constantly revealing through his words and works.

Like other men and women in John's Gospel, Philip invites us to identify with him. His story has our name written on it. Many of us have been with Jesus a long time. How would we answer the question if Jesus were to say to us: 'Have I been with you so long, and yet you do not know me?' Perhaps we might say, 'Yes, Lord, I have been with you a long time.' Yet, which of us could ever say, 'I know you really and truly'?

We all spend a lifetime getting to know Jesus. None of us can ever say, 'Now, I really know Jesus.' But let us pray that, like Philip, we continue to open ourselves up to knowing Jesus. Right through all the time that God gives us, may we continue to grow steadily in our deep and intimate knowledge of Jesus. That is the only thing that ultimately matters – for the apostle Philip long ago and for us today.

In the Gospels, we hear the message of peace at the beginning and at the end of the story of Jesus. When he is born, angels sing the praises of God: 'Glory to God in the highest heaven, and on earth peace among those whom he favours' (Luke 2:14). At the end, before he faces death, Jesus comforts his disciples: 'Peace I leave with you; my peace I give to you' (John 14:27). When he is raised from the dead, he greets his followers: 'Peace be with you' (John 20:19).

The message of peace enfolds the whole story of Jesus. It's no wonder that, when St Paul starts a letter, he regularly comes up with the greeting, 'Grace and *peace* to you from God our Father and the Lord Jesus Christ.'

In the early days of Christianity, Greek served as the common language for the followers of Jesus. They used Greek when they wrote the 27 books of the New Testament. They used Greek for their worship and for many other things, including the inscriptions they commonly put on the tombs of their dear ones who had died and gone home to God: '*en eirēnē* (in peace)'.

Today, many Catholics and other Christians write on graves: '*Requiescat in pace* (RIP) – May he (or she) rest in peace.' We too want peace for our beloved dead. But Jesus wants us to have peace, his peace, here and now in this life and not simply in the life to come. We pray every day at the Eucharist, 'Give us peace (*dona nobis pacem*). Give us peace, your peace, here and now, and hereafter.'

Human beings naturally hunger for peace: peace in their own hearts, peace in their families, peace in the life of their nations, and peace between nations. Human beings agree about the value and beauty of peace. But down the centuries and today, they have constantly disagreed about how peace might come about.

Not far from where I lived in Rome for 33 years, stood the '*Ara pacis*', the altar of peace erected by the Roman emperor Augustus Caesar. His armies and those of his legal father, Julius Caesar, proved efficient machinery for bringing peace to their part of the ancient world. But they did so at the cost of innumerable human lives. Historians have calculated that, when Julius Caesar conquered Gaul (modern France), nearly one million people were killed or carried off into slavery. One can appreciate the comment of the Roman writer Tacitus: 'They make a solitude and they call it peace *(solitudinem faciunt, pacemque appellant)*.'

The message of John's Gospel and the whole of the New Testament stands far apart from the practice of the Caesars and their modern successors. Real peace is a marvellous gift from God. It is *not what we achieve* but *what we receive* as the gift of Christ. It was his gift to us when he moved towards death and rose to new life.

Let us thank the Lord for the wonderful gift of his peace. Let us pray even more sincerely 'Give us peace (*dona nobis pacem*).'

In the month of May, if we were out in the countryside of France, Germany, Italy, Spain, or various regions of the United States, something beautiful would catch our eyes. We would see vineyards growing away furiously in the spring sunshine. In that season, it's marvellous to wander along rows of vines and see them full of life, with fresh, green leaves sprouting everywhere. In the winter the vines are cut back, and look miserable and even dead. But in the spring they send out shoots and quickly become masses of green life.

When he was growing up in Galilee, Jesus saw vineyards in the springtime and the yearly miracle of their fresh life. In John's Gospel, he speaks about our relationship with him as being like branches that grow on a vine (John 15:1-11). When we live with Jesus and in Jesus, we become like those fresh shoots on vines and the masses of green leaves that are so full of life.

Jesus wants us to enjoy wonderful, fresh life in him. With him and in him, it's always springtime. Let's draw our life from him and become like those fresh, green leaves that sprout everywhere on the vines when spring comes.

In the church of San Clemente in Rome, you can marvel at a crucifix set in a mosaic that fills the apse and translates the words of Jesus about his being the vine and our being the branches. As the vine, the crucified Jesus brings life and unity to everyone and everything in a mosaic that embraces the world. His cross is the throne, a throne of victory and life.

At the top of the mosaic, a hand emerges from heaven and crowns the crucified Jesus with a laurel wreath. God has accepted the loving self-sacrifice of Jesus, the great High Priest. At the foot of the cross, a small snake slithers away – a sign of evil being banished by that sacrifice.

Christ has brought life and salvation. Some lively doves, placed along the cross express that. This life and salvation are also symbolised by two deer. They drink water that issues from the cross.

A whole panorama symbolises the world redeemed by Christ and his cross. A woman feeds her chickens; a bird nourishes her young; a man tastes some wine; and several angelic cherubs gambol for joy. Richness and variety fill those scenes. They point to Christ, the vine of life, gathering all creatures to himself and presenting them to the Father.

At the bottom of the apse come two processions of sheep. Six sheep are leaving the town of Bethlehem, and six leaving the city of Jerusalem. They meet in the middle, under the vine that is the cross. They recall the place where Jesus was born, Bethlehem, and the place where he died and rose from the dead, Jerusalem. Bethlehem features a set of descending stairs, while Jerusalem features a window opening on an ascending stairway. That descent and ascent symbolise, of course, how the Son of God stepped down into our world and humbled himself by his suffering on the cross, only to be raised from the dead and return gloriously to the presence of God where he intercedes constantly on our behalf.

The cross of Christ is the tree of life, the vine that brings life to all its branches. More than any cross or crucifix I have ever seen, the mosaic in San Clemente shows how the cross of Christ is utterly life-giving. The whole scene is filled with vibrant activity. Life flows out of the cross. In turn, all life is gathered together by the cross and becomes a supreme gift of praise offered to the Father by Christ, our great and eternal High Priest.

TWENTY-EIGHT

Joy, Friends, Having a Baby, Being One and Being Thomas

For many years during lectures and seminars at the Gregorian University (Rome), I used to spend some time exploring human and divine love. There are so many aspects to love. It is a deep truth that we can never exhaust.

During his last discourse Jesus invites his disciples to 'remain in my love'. He adds at once: 'I have said these things to you so that my *joy* may be in you, and that your *joy* may be complete' (John 15:11). Here Jesus touches on a persistent result of love. Real love always brings joy.

In the story of the prodigal son, the father loves the son and is full of joy when he returns. As he says to his elder son, 'we had to *celebrate and rejoice*, because this brother of yours was dead and has come to life; he was lost and has been found' (Luke 15:32).

True love always brings joy. If the disciples stay in love with Jesus, they will experience something that infallibly comes from love: great joy, even complete joy. There is much more to be said, of course, about love than that it produces real happiness and deep joy. But this is one of love's persistent spin-off effects.

Let us thank Jesus for the love he shares with us. Let us thank him for the peaceful joy and deep happiness his love continues to bring us.

'Faithful friends are a sturdy shelter: whoever finds one has found a treasure. Faithful friends are beyond price; no amount can balance their worth' (Sirach 6:14, 15). What Jesus Ben Sira says has proved itself true innumerable times in human experience. Faithful friends provide us with a shelter right through life. They are a treasure that money can't buy.

That praise of friendship coming from Jesus the son of Sira makes me think of another Jesus, Jesus the son of Mary, our great treasure and our priceless friend.

In John's Gospel, Jesus says to the disciples, 'I have called you friends' (John 15:15). By calling us his friends, he has made us his friends. The words of Jesus have changed our situation forever. 'I have called you friends' is a striking example of what philosophers have described as 'performatives'. These are statements that 'perform' by changing situations, sometimes permanently.

Think of the foreman of a jury returning to the court and saying: 'we find the accused guilty as charged'. Or think of a young woman standing before the altar and saying: 'I take you to be my lawful, wedded husband'. Words like that are much more than mere words that pass through the air and disappear without leaving a trace. These words deeply affect other people and, for better or worse, can even change their lives forever.

That's what happened when Jesus said: 'I have called you friends'. He is our priceless friend, and he has made us his friends for all eternity.

It took Christians a long time to take on board the friendship of Jesus. For many centuries, they seemed to have been happier speaking *of* him and even speaking *to* him as 'Lord', 'Christ', 'Son of God', 'Good Shepherd', 'King of Kings', 'the Word of God' and so forth. Then around the year 1000, a sea change set in with St Anselm of Canterbury, St Bernard of Clairvaux, St Francis of Assisi, Julian of Norwich and others. They started using more personal, deeply affectionate language, calling Jesus their 'Mother', 'Lover' and 'Friend'.

They began taking very seriously what Jesus had said about himself as the mother hen who gathers her chickens under her wings (Luke 13:34). What he said about becoming our friend (John 15:15) and brother (Mark 3:35) grew in influence over them. A lovely medieval prayer to Jesus written by St Richard of Chichester closed with words taken up in the twentieth century by the musical *Godspell*: 'May I know thee more clearly, love thee more dearly, and follow thee more nearly.'

It is worth hearing the whole prayer, which addresses Jesus not merely as our Redeemer but also as our Friend and Brother. 'Thanks be to thee, my Lord Jesus Christ, for all the benefits which thou hast given me, for all the pains and insults thou hast borne for me. O most merciful Redeemer, Friend, and Brother, may I know thee more clearly, love thee more dearly, and follow thee more nearly.'

Jesus is our precious lover, friend, and brother. He is our priceless friend, who joins us on the journey of life and proves always our constant shelter and companion. Jesus, our friend, be with us today and all the days of our lives. May we experience ever more deeply your friendship, and know who you are, our friend forever and ever.

Jesus was not a woman, and so he never had the chance of having a baby. But from growing up in Nazareth, he knew what women went through when giving birth to a baby. He knew the pain and joy that women experience at childbirth. 'When a woman is in labour, she has pain, because her hour has come. But when her child is born, she no longer remembers the anguish because of the joy of having brought a human being into the world' (John 16:21).

Most, if not all, of my readers have visited a young woman just after she has given birth to a child. The hospital room is full of flowers. But THE beautiful thing in the room is the joy on the face of the young mother. You can see her face shining with joy.

Jesus himself, during his years in Nazareth, would have seen the same sight, the face of a young woman simply radiant with joy because she had given birth to a child. He probably saw that many times, and never forgot the shining joy of young mothers.

Jesus thinks of his disciples as going through a similar experience at his death and resurrection. They will first suffer great pain, but then they will be filled with happiness: 'your hearts will rejoice, and no one will take your joy from you' (John 16:22).

Women having babies is something that happens all the time in our world. It might seem an ordinary, normal experience. But Jesus knew how wonderfully special it is, as a woman passes from pain to great joy. He knew too that something like this would be the experience of his disciples. First, they would feel sharp suffering. But then they would experience a unique joy, a joy that no one could ever take away from them.

He wants all of us to be like that, with great happiness in our hearts and radiant joy on our faces. Jesus has gone through this suffering and death on the cross, and is now gloriously risen from the dead. Through his victory over death, he has given us a reason for incredible joy that should constantly light up our faces, a joy that no one can ever take away from us.

Modern democratic societies exhibit a lot of aggressive individualism and unrestrained human self-interest. It is difficult to love your neighbour when the culture encourages you to see your neighbour as your economic rival or even as someone to be exploited. Such autonomous individualism might be summarised: 'If I win, they lose. If they win, I lose.' How can we maintain neighbourly care and fellowship when individuals everywhere are trying to get on, more or less at the expense of others?

Jesus prays: 'Holy Father, protect them ... so that they may be one, as we are one' (John 17:11). With these words, Jesus sets a very high standard for the way his followers should love and be united with one another. Their union with each other should imitate the very way in which Jesus himself is united with the Father and the Holy Spirit.

In the life of the Trinity, the Father, the Son and the Holy Spirit are united with one another in an infinite ecstasy of love. The three divine persons live *with* each other and *for* each other, but never *at the expense of* each other. The divine persons show what our existence should be like: living with each other, living for each other, but never living at the expense of each other.

Jesus prays to his Father that 'they may be one [even] as we are one'. These words set the bar very high. Jesus wants his followers to imitate the very life of God, and to find in the Trinity their primary role model. Jesus wants us to replicate the infinitely loving union that keeps the three divine persons together in an eternal love story, an ecstasy of infinite love. The Trinity shows us what it is to be people in a loving relationship that involves infinite flourishing.

Let us pray that we may be one, even as Jesus, his Father and the Holy Spirit are one. Let us pray that such unity may come in our families, our parishes and the Christian church in our country, so that such peaceful unity may come also to the wider world. The Trinity is nothing less than *the* ideal that sets the standard for humanity. To the extent that the Church reflects the loving communion of God, to that extent society will glimpse what it should become.

What is the picture of Thomas the apostle that John's Gospel offers? Most people think of a sceptic, someone who shrugs his shoulders and is reluctant to believe. He wants hard evidence before he believes in Jesus risen from the dead (John 20:24–29). That is an image of Thomas, shared by many people, including Franco Zeffirelli in *Jesus of Nazareth*.

But there's another portrait of Thomas we might draw from John. Back in Chapter 11, we read of Lazarus falling ill and his two sisters, Martha and Mary, sending word to Jesus about their brother's desperate condition. They lived in Bethany, close to Jerusalem where the authorities had already shown themselves dangerously hostile to Jesus.

The disciples of Jesus warned Jesus against risking another trip into that neighbourhood: 'Rabbi, the Jews were just now trying to stone you, and are you going there again?' (John 11:8). The other disciples were afraid, but not Thomas. He said: 'Let us also go, that we may die with him [Jesus]' (John 11:16).

After the death and burial of Jesus, we read about the other disciples hiding themselves away in a house and locking the doors. They feared the Jewish authorities and would not risk going out on the streets of Jerusalem (John 20:19). But Thomas didn't hide himself with them behind locked doors. He was out and about, showing his face around town. That was why he was missing when Jesus first appeared to the disciples.

Thomas was ready to walk the streets of Jerusalem and courageously face enemies, even death itself. But initially he could not believe in the new life of Jesus risen from the dead. Some, even many, people are like that. They have the courage to risk death but don't have the courage to accept life.

You don't need to be a Christian believer to be brave and face death. Accepting the new life of Christ's resurrection is a great grace, which came to Thomas when he blurted out his confession, 'My Lord and my God!' (John 20:28).

THE ACTS OF THE
APOSTLE AND ST PAUL

TWENTY-NINE

Pentecost, Hearts, Lydia and an Earthquake

'The Holy Ghost is in the fields.' For years those words of Patrick Kavanaugh, an Irish country writer, haunted me. Like him, I had marvelled at the mystery of new life: the fluffy chickens darting across the yard ahead of the hens, the white rings of flowers on the pear trees, and wild rabbits enjoying the grass on an early summer's evening. I still feel a thrill of wonder when I recall all that growth: cows licking their newborn calves, sharp-eyed magpies strutting around with their young, and – not least – peas and beans shooting up through the soil where I had planted seeds in the vegetable garden. But before reading Paddy Kavanaugh, I had never thought of all that fresh life as the work of God's Spirit. Yes, 'the Holy Ghost is in the fields'.

Right from the Book of Genesis, our Scriptures witness to the Spirit of God who initiates life (Genesis 1:2; Psalm 33:6) and stimulates growth. It comes then as no surprise when the risen Jesus breathes on his disciples and says, 'Receive the Holy Spirit' (John 20:22). The life-giving Breath or Spirit of God will animate the tiny community of disciples as the Church begins to live, grow, and move out.

Whether in the fields, in the Church, or in human society, the Holy Spirit is at work, bringing life and growth. That may happen as in the story of the first Pentecost (Acts 2:1–11), with fiery flames, talking in foreign languages, and the sound of a strong, driving wind. Or growth may come as silently as blades of grass springing up from the soil or blossoms opening along the branches of fruit trees.

A wonderful writer and thinker, Tertullian (d. around 225) blessed the early days of the Church. He crafted and promoted some essential language we continue to use: like the term 'Trinity'. He was an old curmudgeon, but we owe a lot to Tertullian. He had his superb, even lyrical, moments, as when he wrote a lovely account of Christian marriage in honour of his wife. When he came to the Trinity, Tertullian introduced several images.

He knew, of course, that his pictures of the Trinity could never hope to be totally successful. There were serious limits to all his pictures. Yet they remain useful. In one of his images for the Trinity, Tertullian spoke of a single, continuous body of water, in which we distinguish three stages. A fountain gives rise to a river, and the river then flows into a canal. I wasn't all that satisfied when I first came across this picture of the Trinity – as the fountain, the river, and the canal. A fountain and a river can be clean, bright and wonderful. But a canal! Canals move along so slowly, and they can be dirty and smelly. But then, I thought, a canal brings water right there into the fields; it could become a good image for the Holy Spirit. Yes, a fountain and a river are fine. But you also need a canal which brings the water where it is needed – into the fields where it makes the crops grow and fruit trees blossom. What canals do is truly life-giving; so three cheers for Tertullian and his image of the Trinity as fountain, river and canal!

The Holy Spirit makes so many things possible, and makes so many things happen: our personal faith as Christians, the forgiveness of sins, the life that comes through the sacraments, the Church's basic fidelity to the original good news that is Christ himself, and a loving communion between groups and individuals where previously all communication seems to have broken down. Everywhere the Spirit of God is at work, humanising, gracing and giving life to people within Christianity and beyond.

In the sacrament of reconciliation, the prayer of absolution acknowledges how the Holy Spirit has been 'sent among us for the forgiveness of sins'. The Third Eucharistic Prayer, after recognising how 'all life' and 'all holiness' come through the working of the Holy Spirit, calls for the descent of the Spirit: 'And so Father, we bring you these gifts. We ask you to make them holy by the power of your Spirit, that they may become the body and blood of your Son, our Lord Jesus Christ, at whose command we celebrate this Eucharist.' These two examples, taken from the sacrament of penance and the Mass typify ways in which Roman Catholics and other Christians acknowledge the Spirit of God as communicating life, holiness, and growth to wounded believers and human beings.

The life-giving power of the Holy Spirit is something like the power of love. Those who experience love know what it is, but have difficulty describing it to the satisfaction of others. 'You just know' was the answer one mother gave her young daughter when the child asked 'How do you know when you love someone?' At the time, Mary considered the answer disappointing and unsatisfactory. She wanted a sharply clear reply and precise guidelines. Years later she thought: 'How right and wise my mother was to give me none.' Attempts to describe and define the Holy Spirit are no less difficult. Neither God the Father nor God the Son presents quite the same problem as God the Holy Spirit.

After Mary recalled what her mother had said, the line of an old song came into my mind: 'Oh, sweet mystery of love, I know you now.' The Holy Spirit is '*the* sweet mystery of divine love' that binds together the Father and the Son in an ecstasy of love and proves the mystery of divine love at work everywhere in our Church and our world.

Centuries ago, Spanish navigators called the island-continent of Australia 'The Land of the Holy Spirit'. That name has always made me think of what happens when heavy rain comes to the centre of Australia. Within a few weeks, under the blazing sun, plants spring up, flowers bloom, birds return, and the deep mud beneath dried up lakes produces fish in abundance. The desert comes alive. What happens in the dead heart of Australia highlights in a startling fashion the life and growth that the Spirit of God makes possible everywhere. Not only Australia but also the entire planet could be called 'the World of the Holy Spirit', the world in which the mystery of love that is the Spirit is ceaselessly and mysteriously at work to bring fresh life and new growth.

The use of the terms 'Holy *Spirit*' and the old-fashioned 'Holy *Ghost*' may be part of the difficulty in our understanding. Spirits and ghosts are elusive beings, with no material existence, experienced by some and discredited by others.

We have our images for the Holy Spirit: the dove, a canal, wind, fire and a sudden burst of light. We use images that range from gentleness to overwhelming power, from peaceful quiet to deafening noise. Whatever image we prefer, the Holy Spirit means transformation and growth.

At the first Pentecost, the Spirit inspired those ordinary Galileans, forced them out of their room in Jerusalem, and sent them fearlessly across the then-known world. That great manifestation of power at Pentecost could make us think back to the first verses of the Bible: 'In the beginning when God created the heavens and the earth, the earth was a formless void and darkness covered the face of the deep, while the Spirit of God swept over the face of the waters' (Genesis 1:1, 2). Rich life and exuberant growth were about to start. The Spirit of God was present to bring all the life and growth that set the world going and eventually the Church.

'And God, who knows the human heart, testified to [the Gentiles] by giving them the Holy Spirit, just as he did to us' (Acts 15:8). These words of Simon Peter at the Council of Jerusalem refer directly to the Roman centurion, Cornelius. The Holy Spirit came down upon Cornelius, his friends and his family before they received baptism (Acts 10:44-48). Peter witnessed an outpouring of the Holy Spirit upon those who were not yet baptised. That experience of the presence and power of the Holy Spirit beyond the community of Christian believers proved very important for Peter and the other leaders of the Church gathered for a council in Jerusalem (Acts 15:1–29).

The Spirit is also powerfully active beyond the Church and among all people – mysteriously, but really, there in all human hearts. It's easy to recognise the Holy Spirit present in our fellow Christians or at least some of them. But, like Peter, we should learn to recognise the power and presence of the Spirit in all people who make up our world. They themselves may not be aware of the Spirit's powerful presence. But the Spirit is there in the lives of everyone. When we meet any human being, we meet someone in whose life the Holy Spirit is wonderfully, albeit mysteriously, active.

Let us pray to share some of the faith in the Spirit that Peter learned. If we come to believe strongly in the universal presence of the Holy Spirit, it will change forever the way we look at all human beings and our world.

Paul's initial missionary journey into Europe began in Philippi, where his first convert was a woman called Lydia (Acts 16:11–15). She listened to what Paul was saying, and the Lord 'opened her heart'. She and her household came to faith and were baptised – the first converts in Europe that we know about.

Paul preached the good news. That was, so to speak, the 'external word'. But there was also the 'internal word': the Lord opened her heart. Faith came from hearing both the outer word and the inner word.

Nowadays we hear so many outer words. The internet, television, the papers and social media bring us a constant barrage of words. They also include life-giving words from Pope Francis and others who bring us the good news. Far more than Lydia, we are swamped with words: good, bad, and indifferent. More than ever, we need the Lord to open our hearts and let us hear him speaking within us. Unless the Lord opens our hearts, we will miss all those good words spoken or written to us. They are there for us in the outer world, but can fail to have their grace-filled impact. Lord, open our hearts and let us hear you and those who speak for you.

In Acts 16:19–34, we hear an amazing story of God working at top speed, through Paul and Silas, to bring salvation to a jailer and his whole family. What were the jailer and his family like? We have no idea. We are only told that, after Paul and Silas had been flogged, the jailer put them into the most secure part of his prison, chained them up, and went off to bed.

Then about midnight an earthquake threw all the doors of the jail open and knocked the chains off Paul, Silas and the other prisoners. The jailer woke up, and thought everyone had escaped. Faced with the obvious charge of failing terribly in his duty, he was about to commit suicide. But Paul stopped him doing so.

The jailer led Paul and Silas out of the prison. Unexpectedly he asked them the only question that ultimately matters: 'what must I do to be saved?' Notice how at this point he asked only about himself. But his two Christian prisoners thought in the plural: 'Become a believer in the Lord Jesus and you will be saved, and your household too' (own translation). All the members of the jailer's family got up and gathered around Paul and Silas. The two Christian leaders proceeded to preach the good news to the man and his family.

In the early hours of the morning, the jailer then washes the wounds of Paul and Silas. There is water available.

So Paul and Silas use it to baptise the jailer and his family and make them members of the people of God. The family all finish up celebrating their conversion with an early morning meal.

What an amazing story of God acting at high speed and late at night for some not very devout people, the keeper of the town jail and his whole family! It's the most extraordinary story I've ever read about an earthquake proving a unique blessing for some people and doing so at great speed, hardly before the buildings have stopped shaking. In a few short hours, God turns an earthquake and a jail break into a story of grace and conversion.

We simply cannot put limits to the speed with which God may bring exceptional blessings. God can do things for us in the space of a few hours, and do so in the most unlikely circumstances.

THIRTY

Freedom, Resurrection, Love and Faith

Reaching the heart of his Letter to the Romans, Paul speaks repeatedly of freedom, about God setting us free from slavery and giving us the freedom and glory of his sons and daughters (Romans 8:1–17). God means freedom, real freedom. But many people disagree with what Paul says. They think of the issue as a choice: either God or freedom. For many people, the more God comes into our lives, the less freedom we have. But Paul insists. God means freedom.

When we reflect on our experience, we can find reasons for agreeing with Paul. Are the people who leave God out of their lives really free? Do they truly enjoy more genuine freedom than those who keep God in the centre of their lives?

During my lifetime I have been blessed by knowing some men and women who were heroically holy and truly saints. I was lucky enough, for example, to know Mother Teresa of Calcutta. She was very close to God, and she was also clearly a very free person. Being close to God took nothing away from her freedom. In fact, being close to God seemed to have made her an even freer individual.

Let us pray that we may always embrace God, the One who gives us freedom and dignity, the God who wants us to be always his free sons and daughters.

'He who raised Christ from the dead will give life to your mortal bodies' (Romans 8:11). Here Paul speaks of the promise that the God, who has raised Jesus, will also raise us from the dead. Yes, we believe and hope that we too will be raised from the dead. But what will our bodily resurrection be like? Can we make any informed guesses about our coming resurrection from the dead?

Various things that we now know may help us explore this hope for resurrection. We know, for instance, how changeable our bodies are. There is a constant and huge interchange of matter between our bodies and our environment, as we discard old matter and absorb new matter into our bodily existence. Our bodies seem more like a flowing river that is constantly changing, rather than something fixed and stable that God could raise from the dead. Our bodies are a passing parade of millions of molecules that at different moments constitute our particular, physical existence. What then could the resurrection of our body look like?

We might help ourselves here with a classic truism: we are what we do. We can adapt this saying and declare, 'In the resurrection we will be what we have done.' Or better still, 'In the resurrection, we will be what we have freely done in and through our bodies.'

Let me explain. When each of us does (and suffers) various things, we make our own history or at least a part of that history. We do things and freely create our history *with our bodies*. My writing this page with my hands and my readers reading this page with their eyes become part of the history of each one of us. We freely do this writing and this reading, and do so with our bodies. If we didn't have a body, we couldn't freely do such things and go on creating our own history.

Thinking this way allows us to picture the resurrection of our body to be the resurrection of our *bodily history*. We will be raised with and as the bodily history that we have made in this life. In the resurrection, that bodily history which has made up the unique story of each person will be brought to a new and transformed life. Noting of the unique story that has made each one of us will be lost. Our risen existence will express what we as embodied persons were and what we became in our earthly life.

The resurrection of our body will be the resurrection of the history that we have freely made with our bodies. We will be what we have done in and through our bodies. In these terms we can see how our bodies and the embodied history we create with these bodies matter enormously. Our individual bodily history will be raised and transformed to live with God forever and ever.

Most people treasure the wonderful passage of love that Paul crafted in 1 Corinthians: 'Love is patient; love is kind; love is not envious or boastful or arrogant', and so forth (1 Corinthians13:4–8). The heart of this hymn is a beautiful statement about what love does for others and what, for their sake, love refrains from doing.

The statement is even more powerful in the Greek language Paul uses. Writing in that language, Paul brings in 16 verbs: 'love acts in a patient way; love acts in a kind way; love never gives way to jealousy; love does not indulge in boasting', and so on.

Well, what's the difference? In any language, verbs are dynamic; verbs express actions, events that are happening. Love acts in this way or that way.

Some of these verbs can be readily translated into English as verbs: 'Love believes all things; love hopes all things; love endures all things; love never ends.' But some of the Greek verbs of Paul are normally not translated into English as verbs. Instead of 'love acts in a patient way', we normally read: 'love is patient'. Instead of 'love acts in a kind way', we normally read: 'love is kind'. By not keeping the verbs, we may lose a little of the dynamic quality of love that Paul writes about.

Love is a verb. It exists in action. Love is not a thing we can store in a cupboard and bring out for dusting every now and then. No, love between people exists in action, right here and now. Love is verbal, or it doesn't exist at all. The 16 verbs that Paul uses express something essential about love: it is something that happens, and happens many times.

Notice too that Paul writes about love in the *present* tense – that is to say, about love acting here and now. Love acts here and now in a patient way; love acts here and now in a kind way. Love here and now believes all things. Love here and now endures all things. Love is not something that happened yesterday, or will happen tomorrow or sometime in the future. Love acts and exists as a present reality.

That's Paul's lovely vision of love. It's a dynamic activity, something always in action in the here and now. May we all have the courage to let love become something always in action, here and now in our daily lives.

Some years ago, a journalist friend of mine was invited to address a large gathering of clergy, and was looking around for a key message to give them. When he telephoned, I said, 'Tell them to put their hand in the hand of the man from Galilee, and tell them to keep it there.' For good measure, I added: 'Yes, it is an evangelical message, but that doesn't stop it from being the best policy in life.'

What I might have added was that this advice reflects what Paul wrote: ' . . . we walk by faith and not by sight' (2 Corinthians 5:7). We are all exiles from our true home, and faith is a journey on which we walk home with the Lord Jesus. He is our life coach as we travel towards our final, utterly worthwhile destination. Without a deep and regular relationship with him in prayer, we will not make the journey with the peace, persistence, and inner joy that he wants us to enjoy.

Paul was at his sensitive best in choosing the verb 'walk'. Faith is, after all, something essentially 'verbal' or dynamic. Like love, faith is not a treasured object that we store in a closet and bring out occasionally for a good polish. Faith is a living activity that *happens*, like walking hand in hand through the twilight with someone whom we love and trust unconditionally.

As regards the dynamic, lived quality of faith, another leading New Testament writer converges with Paul, even if he makes the point in a different way. In his Gospel, John always employs the verb 'to believe' and never the noun 'faith'. When you count the occurrences of 'to believe', you will find John using the verb 98 times. The whole point of his Gospel is to help people believe in Jesus. Just in case any readers have missed the point, at the end John addresses them directly and insists: 'These are written so that you may come to *believe* that Jesus is the Christ, the Son of God, and that through *believing* you may have life in his name' (John 20:31 emphasis added).

For John, faith is an ongoing relationship with Jesus that feeds us and gives us real *life*, both here and hereafter. In this context the Gospel makes another significant choice, this time between two possible words for 'life'. It never uses *'bios'* (from which we get 'biology' or the science of life) but always *'zōē'* (from which we get 'zoology' or the science of animal life). What's the difference for John? He wants to indicate that believing in Jesus does not bring us merely organic life. We have that anyway. What Jesus shares with us is something much more valuable: the deep life of the Holy Spirit, the 'spiritual' life that we receive even now and that will last forever. 'Those who believe in me', Jesus declares, 'already have eternal life and will live for all eternity' (John 6:40, 47 own translation).

As our life coach, Jesus does something that ordinary life coaches cannot do. When we walk with him on the journey of faith, he not only shows us the right road but also gives us the vitality needed to make that journey. He is the very 'bread of life' for all pilgrims who have come to believe in him and follow him.

On the eve of Pentecost Sunday a few years back, a dear friend of mine died from a cancer that had spread from his lungs to other parts of his body. Simon's children were all there at his bedside, and his wife held his hand as he made the final leap into eternal life. A personal relationship with Jesus had given Simon a steady strength and direction. He had come from God, and now he was going home to God. It was all as simple and beautiful as that.

Simon loved Isabel, cherished their four children and those they have married, and doted on his eight grandchildren. Physically powerful and handsome, he was always an amusing companion and endlessly generous to those in distress. Simon went through life drawing his boundless spiritual energy and rock-hard hope from the faith that Jesus kept burning in him right to the end.

Simon's death at the age of 69 was, of course, a painful blow to Isabel and his family. But we all saw in him a striking witness to what enduring faith in Jesus brings in this life and beyond. Simon did life proud, and, when he came to leave this world, he did death proud.

What we can also say is that faith in Jesus gave constant meaning to Simon's life. Without such faith, people can be left desperately asking themselves: 'What's it all about?' In good times and bad times, it is faith in Jesus that constantly shows us what it's all about. Believing in him does not take away the pain and hurt of life. But this faith allows us to glimpse a deep meaning, which makes mysterious sense of what we experience and which will always keep us walking with Jesus on our way home to God.

THIRTY-ONE

Hardships, the Philippians and Number One

'My grace is sufficient for you, for power is made perfect in weakness' (2 Corinthians 12:9). 2 Corinthians, the closest Paul ever came to writing an autobiography, describes at length his 'weakness', or the way in which his missionary life was incessantly threatened and afflicted.

The encouragement that the risen Lord offers Paul, when the apostle was overburdened and even crushed by various hardships, comes across as very different from the ideals of the Greek world in which the apostle had grown up.

In that world a personal 'sufficiency' that could rise above hardships and simply set them aside is idealised. We hear something similar coming through the modern saying, 'When the going gets tough, the tough get going.' A current tattoo chips in with the advice, 'If you are going through hell, keep going.'

Prompted by the Lord, Paul does not, however, set sufferings aside and 'tough it out'. He accepts his weakness because he now appreciates the value of his afflictions. They reveal and mediate the very power of God.

As we all know, what Paul wrote can be subtle, deep, and even downright mysterious. It's because of his subtlety that he has provided plenty of work for brilliant scholars. Yet he can also prove wonderfully straightforward and simple. He writes to the Philippians: 'And this is my prayer, that your love may overflow more and more with knowledge and full insight to help you to determine what is best, so that in the day of Christ you may be pure and blameless' (Philippians 1:9, 10).

The community of Christians in Philippi was the first local church that Paul founded when he crossed over from Asia to Europe. The apostle showed enormous affection for the Philippians and they for him. That mutual love shone out when Paul began by thanking God for the Philippians and praying for them (Philippians 1:3–11). Notice how often in these verses he used 'I', 'me', and 'my' (twelve times), and the number of times he used 'you' and 'your' (eleven times). He did that right from the start: '*I* thank *my* God every time *I* remember *you*, constantly praying with joy in every one of *my* prayers for all of *you*' (Philippians 1: 3, 4 emphasis added). It was a matter not just of a richly personal language but also of a deep personal love, which Paul felt for the entire community in Philippi.

No abstract, doctrinal treatise, the Letter to the Philippians is concerned with what Paul has experienced and what he wants to do with the rest of his life. He reminds his beloved community of the one, great passion at the heart of his existence: 'For to me, to live is Christ' (Philippians 1:21 NIV). His life is utterly devoted to Christ; it is from Christ that he draws everything. His life is no longer his own; it has been taken over by the Lord: 'Christ Jesus has made [Paul] his own' (Philippians 3:12). Paul now wears himself out, telling people about Jesus, bringing people to Jesus, and sharing with them his own passionate love for Jesus. The apostle shows us what a Jesus-centred existence looks like. In living or dying, all that matters to Paul is being taken up into the life of the risen Lord: 'I want to know Christ and the power of his resurrection and the sharing of his sufferings by becoming like him in his death, if somehow I may attain the resurrection from the dead' (Philippians 3:10, 11).

As the letter draws to a close, Paul assures the Philippians: 'I can do all things through him who strengthens me' (Philippians 4:13). This is an extraordinarily confident statement from the apostle. He is serenely confident that he can do, not just some things, but all things, because Christ is there to strengthen him. The trust and assurance of the apostle can take your breath away.

Paul is not talking about mere theory and brave hopes. He speaks rather of his personal experience. Time in and time out, he has experienced how he can do all things in and through Christ. He trusts that this experience will continue.

'In Christ' points to the place where Paul finds himself. He lives totally united with Christ. The 'in him who strengthens me' points to the agent who empowers Paul, Christ himself. Paul can do all things, because he does them though the powerful agency of Christ.

Let us pray that we might share some of the confidence of Paul. We shouldn't set any limits on what Christ can do in and through us. We too are united with him. He is our 'place', the place where we live. Hence we too can say with utter truth and complete trust: 'I can do all things in him who strengthens me'.

Many scholars maintain that Paul is citing a hymn in the first chapter of Colossians. This hymn celebrates Christ as being the firstborn *over* all creation and the firstborn *from* the dead (Colossians 1:15–20). We might express today the same faith by saying, 'Jesus is Lord, Jesus is King, Jesus is our everything'. Please read the hymn before you continue with my comments.

Both as creator and as redeemer, Christ is number one. He is supreme both in the order of creation and in the order of redemption. To express the universal supremacy of Christ, the hymn uses the word 'all' eight times. He is the firstborn over *all* creation, for in him *all* things were created. *All* things have been created through him and for him. He himself is before *all* things, and in him *all* things have held together. He is the firstborn from the dead, so that in *all* things he might be number one. In him *all* the fullness of God was pleased to dwell. Through him God was pleased to reconcile to himself *all* things. Thus eight times the hymn celebrates Christ being supreme over all things.

The hymn says the equivalent by speaking of Christ being supreme over the things visible and invisible and, twice, of his being supreme over the things in the heavens and on earth. The hymn becomes an extraordinary celebration of Christ being universally supreme.

It turns very easily into personal prayer. We can speak to Christ: 'You are the image of the unseen God. You are the firstborn over all creation. In you all things in heaven and earth were created,' and so forth. We can sum up the whole hymn by saying with joy and gratitude: 'Jesus is Lord, Jesus is King and Jesus is our everything.'

THIRTY-TWO

A Heavenly Perspective, Praying Always and Taking Things for Granted

'So if you have been raised with Christ, seek the things that are above, where Christ is, seated at the right hand of God. Set your minds on things that are above . . . you have died, and your life is hidden with Christ in God. When Christ who is your life is revealed, then you also will be revealed with him in glory' (Colossians 3:1–4).

We live our lives within a certain perspective. We can also say we live our lives from a certain standpoint. A perspective means looking at things from a certain angle, and taking a particular view of things. A standpoint involves standing somewhere and also seeing things in our own particular way.

The passage from Colossians invites us to maintain an extraordinary perspective when we live out our lives. It wants us to look at our existence in the world from an unusual angle and take a remarkable view of where we are and what we can expect.

Paul asks us to take a heavenly perspective on things, and set our minds on Christ who is risen from the dead and taken up into heavenly glory. That should be our constant standpoint, with our eyes fixed on Jesus in his glory and seeing everything from that perspective.

This sketch of the perspective or standpoint that should characterise Christian life can turn ever so easily into personal prayer of faith and hope. 'I have been raised with Christ. Let me seek the things that are above, where Christ my Saviour is seated at the right hand of God. Let me set my mind on heavenly things. Jesus, I have died and my life is hidden with you, in God. You are my life. When you are revealed, I will be revealed with you in glory.'

Some of my readers may have read *The Way of a Pilgrim*. It's the story of a Russian pilgrim who suffers from a withered arm and who meets with all kinds of calamities. His house burns down, and his wife and child die. He decides to go on a pilgrimage.

He sets out with a shoulder bag containing some bread and a copy of the Bible. In the Bible, he reads 'pray without ceasing' (1 Thessalonians 5:17). The pilgrim then begins to search for someone who will teach him to pray without ceasing. He goes from one priest to another, and hears beautiful sermons on prayer. But no one teaches him how to pray.

Sometimes he would go to a priest and put the question directly: 'How can I pray without ceasing?' One priest said: 'God will teach you how to pray.' Another priest told him: 'Any time you do the will of God, you are praying. And if you do the will of God constantly, you are always praying.'

This continued until one day the pilgrim found a monk and told him: 'I am seeking somebody who will teach me how to pray constantly'. The monk answered: 'Give great thanks to God, because he has sent you someone who will teach you how to pray constantly.'

He took the pilgrim by the hand and told him, 'Say "Lord Jesus Christ, Son of God, have mercy on me" 500 times.' The next day the monk told him to repeat this prayer 1000 times, then 2000 times, and so on. While the pilgrim was learning how to pray, his spiritual father died. The pilgrim went to his tomb and burst into tears: 'God gave me someone to teach me how to pray constantly, and now he has taken him away. God, help me to manage on my own.'

The pilgrim took up his shoulder bag but this time he took along with him a famous, old book, the *Philocalia*, a treatise on the prayer of the heart or the Jesus prayer, which he had been learning. As the pilgrim read the *Philocalia*, he began to put the Jesus prayer into his heart. After a while, his heart took over the prayer and began to say the prayer.

Then one morning the pilgrim woke up, and found that he was no longer saying the Jesus prayer but that his heart was saying the prayer. He had learned to pray continuously. As his heart kept beating, the prayer was being said. Whether he was talking, walking or doing other things, the Jesus prayer went on.

I have told this story of the Jesus prayer not only because of the advice of Paul ('pray without ceasing') but also because of the example of the blind beggar in Mark 10:46–52 ('Jesus, Son of David, have mercy on me'). In different forms that prayer has become the prayer of millions of Christians. It can also become the prayer of our hearts.

The first reading for the twenty-third Sunday of ordinary time in Year C is taken from the Book of Wisdom 9:13–18. It begins by asking: 'Who can know the intentions of God? Who can discern the will of the Lord?' The anonymous author of this book knows how very hard it can be to know the intentions of God and discern the will of the Lord. He remarks, 'The reasoning of mortals is unsure, and our intentions unstable.'

Thus the Book of Wisdom talks frankly about the difficulty of knowing the intentions and will of God. An extraordinary example of this difficulty turns up in the second reading (Philemon 9, 10, 12–17). Paul is now old and in prison. A slave, Onesimus, has run away from his owner, Philemon, and made his way to Paul.

Even though the apostle is a prisoner, he is able to look after the runaway slave, both spiritually and materially. Onesimus decides to become a Christian, and Paul has evidently baptised him. And then Paul realises that he should send the runaway slave back to his owner. Paul has done just that, but he has also written a letter for Onesimus to deliver to his owner, Philemon. On that twenty-third Sunday in Year C we hear a large section read from the letter.

The whole letter breathes gentleness and kindness, but it's quite clear what Paul desires for Onesimus. He wants Philemon not to punish Onesimus but to release him from his status as a slave. To bring that about, Paul has written a beautiful, even tender letter. There is an ancient tradition that Philemon did just what Paul asked. He gave Onesimus his freedom, and the former slave became a church leader.

Some scholars have speculated that, in gratitude for what had happened to him, Onesimus gathered the letters of St Paul. By the end of the first century some Christian or Christians had, in fact, collected the apostle's letters. Who could have been more motivated to do that than Onesimus, whose life had been so blessed by the old apostle? It's a beautiful letter, the Letter to Philemon, and a beautiful, early tradition about what happened to Onesimus. But there's one, central point missing.

It never occurred to Paul that God does not intend slavery. Paul simply took for granted the institution of slavery. The apostle was a very brilliant and utterly holy follower of Jesus. But he couldn't or at least didn't reason his way through to realising that the institution of slavery was against the divine will. All human beings are created in the very image and likeness of God. This means that, for God, there can be no first-class citizens, owners of slaves, and second-class citizens, the slaves themselves. Paul believed that every human being is made in the image and likeness of God. But he could not see or at least did not see how this belief simply ruled out slavery as intrinsically wrong.

Now I say all this not to belittle Paul or cut him down to size. For me personally and for innumerable other Christians, he has proved himself a wonderful spiritual guide, one who has led so many people into following Jesus and finding how blessed it is to live with and in the risen Christ. Nevertheless, even Paul could remain blinkered about the institution of slavery. That leaves me with the daunting questions: are there things in my life about which I remain blinkered, things that I simply take for granted but which are intrinsically wrong? Are there things in our society or in our Church that we perhaps never question but which are not according to the will of God? Even though he never intended this, Paul's Letter to Philemon leaves us with just that challenge.

LETTERS OF ST PETER
AND THE BOOK
OF REVELATION

THIRTY-THREE

Hope, Love and Sharing God's Life

'Reverence the Lord Jesus in your hearts, and always have your answer ready for people who ask you the reason for the hope that you have' (1 Peter 3:15 own translation).

Have you ever thought about the way our hopes keep us going? Day by passing day, we rise in the morning, have breakfast, and keep going because our hopes motivate us. We get out of bed because we hope that this day will be a good one, or at least a tolerably happy one.

We have our hopes for ourselves; we have our hopes for our children and others who are dear to us. We have our hopes for the business where we work, and hopes for the church where we worship. All kinds of hopes keep us going, day in and day out.

We may have to put up with all manner of difficulties. We may have to cope with a variety of sufferings – with the pain that other people bring us and with the pain our own bodies bring us. But we keep going because we hope that God and other people will bless us. Somehow things will work out OK. Hopes form the engine of our lives. Our hopes keep us moving down the road of life, moving more quickly or maybe moving more slowly. We all need our hopes to get us out of bed in the morning and keep us going in our daily lives.

I have been talking about our hopes in the plural, all those particular hopes about our personal relationships, our work, our health, and the rest. Peter speaks of hope in the singular, about the great hope that we share. We reverence the Lord Jesus in our hearts, and he is the great hope for our lives. He is THE hope that makes sense of particular, smaller hopes and gives meaning to them.

We reverence the Lord Jesus who says to each of us, 'I will come again and will take you to myself, so that where I am, there you may be also' (John 14:3). Those are among the most beautiful words in the whole Bible, the most consoling promise we might imagine. That's the great hope that holds together and makes sense of all the smaller, particular hopes that fill our lives.

Some critics want to dismiss this hope for final life beyond death, life with Jesus forever and ever, as the opium of the people. This great hope is not opium; it's dynamite. The hope that Jesus will take each of us to himself is like a stick of dynamite that has gone off some distance behind us, blows us joyfully in the future, and keeps us going vigorously along the road of life.

Yes, let us hang onto all our smaller hopes. But let us never forget the GREAT hope that holds everything together and gives power and meaning to our smaller hopes. We treasure the Lord Jesus in our hearts, because we know his promise: 'I will come again and will take you to myself, so that where I am, there you may be also.'

'Love one another deeply from the heart' (1 Peter 1:22). 1 Peter expects a great deal from the holy people of God. As we might say, this letter sets the bar very high. To set the bar high is something that happens in the Olympic Games for those who take part in high jumping or pole vaulting. The bar goes up, and the athletes try to jump over the new height.

1 Peter has already set the bar very high by reminding the people of their being called by God: 'as he who called you is holy, be holy yourselves in all your conduct' (1 Peter 1:15). The readers of this letter are invited to imitate the very holiness of God: be holy as God himself is holy.

Next comes an unqualified call to love: 'Love one another *deeply* from the heart.' The verse could also be translated: 'Love one another *constantly* from the heart.' Either way, that also sets the bar very high. Loving deeply, constantly, and from the heart requires a huge leap on our part. But that's what Peter expects of us.

Both 1 Peter 1:22 and 1 Peter 1:15 can seem very hard, even impossibly hard to practice. How can I manage to love others deeply, constantly and from my heart? By myself, I cannot possibly do that. Only Jesus can make that possible. After all, he came 'not to be served but to serve' (Mark 10:45). He can give each of us the strength to leap that high, serving others and loving them deeply and constantly.

1 Peter is a wonderful letter, which sets the bar very high for Christian behaviour. Jesus will help us to jump that high and reach the height of that bar.

'He has given . . . his precious and very great promises, so that through them . . . you may become participants of the divine nature' (2 Peter 1:4).

Many Christians don't care to read 2 Peter, being put off by its warnings against false teachers. But that means missing such gems as sharing in the very nature of God. St Athanasius, the famous Christian leader in Alexandria, treasured that verse. He helped many later Christians to recognise what God has done by making us 'participants of the divine nature'.

As far as God is concerned, nothing is too good for us. The greatest good thing that God could imaginably give us is a share in the very divine life and nature. That's just what God has done for us through Jesus Christ. Sharing in the nature of God is the best thing that we could possibly imagine God doing for us. And that is what God has done – for each one of us.

THIRTY-FOUR

Newness and Listening to the Scriptures

'Then I saw a new heaven and a new earth; for the first heaven and the first earth had passed away' (Revelation 21:1).

Recently I saw a TV ad for a new brand of car, with other young people milling around the owner and a slogan very much in evidence, 'a lifetime of new mates'. Of course, no car can guarantee a lifetime of 'new mates'. Yet the ad reminded me of a central truth: right from the time we were babies, we human beings naturally love new things.

Children love new toys. When we grow up, we treasure all kinds of new things. A new job can give us a fresh start in life. What's new can seem wonderful, almost magical, and always very welcome: a new dress, a new car, a new face around the office, a new baby born to our daughter, the coming of the New Year. You can think of the many ways that something or someone new can fill us with delight. What's new can prove sheer bliss.

The Book of Revelation, as much as any book in the Bible, pictures God as constantly doing new things for us and giving us a fresh start. God promises a new heaven and a new earth; our whole world and we ourselves will be made wonderfully new by our God. But, even now, God promises: 'I am making all things new' (Revelation 21:5) – not just some things and some people, but all things and all people. God, even now, constantly wants to make a new people of us.

How God will go about making the new heaven and the new earth remains very mysterious. But the promise has been made. God will make our world and us wonderfully new. That new heaven and new earth will fill us with deep delight and everlasting happiness. With joy and gratitude, let us sing a new song unto the Lord.

Years ago, before and after the Second Vatican Council (1962–5), a German Redemptorist, Fr Bernard Häring, wrote a great deal in the areas of moral theology and spirituality. He had many valuable things to say, and interesting images to use.

Once I heard him remark that we all need what he called 'spiritual hearing aids', so that we can hear what God says to us. God speaks to us constantly: through the inspired and inspiring Scriptures, through the Eucharist, in private prayer, through what other people say, and so forth. But we don't always listen to God. We need spiritual hearing aids.

That's another way of expressing what Jesus says to us in the Gospels: 'Pay attention to what you hear' (Mark 4:24). We ought to become good listeners, to one another and to God.

This book is aimed at opening up for its readers further ways of listening to the Scriptures. Every now and then we can hear or read some passage of Scripture and it hits us. We feel, 'these words have my name on them'.

Way back in the fourth century, a passage of Matthew's Gospel did just that for a young man in Egypt. His parents had died recently, and he had to look after his sister. Then in church he heard the words: 'If you wish to be perfect, go, sell your possessions, and give the money to the poor, and you will have treasure in heaven; then come, follow me' (Matthew 19:21). The invitation came home to him. He felt, 'these words have my name written on them'. He sold his property, made provision for his sister, gave the rest of the proceeds to the poor, and became a hermit. He entered history as St Antony the Hermit, one of the founders of Christian monastic life.

Antony is a spectacular example of someone who truly listened to the Scriptures, took them to heart and acted on them. He was a good listener to God, and paid attention to what he heard. May we too have our spiritual hearing aids, to hear the word of God, take it to heart, and constantly act on it.

A couple of centuries after Antony, Pope Gregory the Great said that the Scriptures are like waters in which lambs may walk and elephants swim. In other words, in the Scriptures there is something there for everyone: for little lambs and great, big elephants. Whether we are lambs or elephants we can all relate to the Scriptures and draw from them refreshment and life.

Index of Names

Biblical Index

‹